MW00626262

UNF*CKABLEWITH

Rising From the Ashes Into Your
BLACK WOMAN BADASSERY

CATRICE M. JACKSON
INTERNATIONAL BEST-SELLING AUTHOR

Published by Catriceology Enterprises, LLC
Omaha, NE | United States of America
Copyright © 2019 by Catrice M. Jackson

ALL RIGHTS RESERVED No portion of this publication may be reproduced, stored in any electronic system, or transmitted in any form or by any means, electronic, mechanical, photocopy, recording, or otherwise, without written permission from the author. Brief quotations may be used in literary reviews.

The author has made every effort to ensure the accuracy of the information within this book was correct at the time of publication. The author does not assume and hereby disclaims any liability to any party for any loss, damage, or disruption caused by errors or omissions, whether such errors or omissions result from accident, negligence, or any other cause.

FOR INFORMATION CONTACT: Catrice M. Jackson, M.S., LMHP, LPC, Global Visionary Leader of the Awakened Conscious Shift, Racial Justice Educator, Speaker, and International Best-Selling Author.

Online ordering is available for all products. www.amazon.com
Website: www.catriceology.com

ISBN-13: 9780983839866 (Catriceology Enterprises, LLC)
ISBN-10: 0-9838398-6-7

Book Cover Design: Kerri Liu
Book Cover Photography: Monica Sempek | Monica Sempek Photography
Editor: Marian Gallagher
Interior Design: Kerri Liu

Printed in the USA 10 9 8 7 6 5 4 3 2

This book is a memoir; thus, the events, people, locales, and conversations described within are based on the author's memories and are not meant to be exact depictions. In addition, the author has in many cases purposely changed or omitted certain details to protect the privacy of the individuals.

This book also contains the opinions and ideas of its author and other third parties, and is not intended as a substitute for medical, health, psychological, or any other kind of personal professional services. If the reader requires personal, medical, health, or other assistance or advice, a competent professional should be consulted.

The author and publisher specifically disclaim all responsibility for any liability, loss, or risk, personal or otherwise, that is incurred as a consequence, directly or indirectly, of the use and application of the contents of this book.

UNF*CKABLEWITH

Rising From the Ashes Into Your
BLACK WOMAN BADASSERY

TABLE OF CONTENTS

UNF*CKABLEWITH
Rising From the Ashes Into Black Woman Badassery

DEDICATION

THE MATRIARCHS

Dottie J. Hardgraves (Noel)
Maternal Matriarch: Grandmother
Ancestor since 2010

* * * * * * * *

Dear Gran,
I miss you. I love you.
Thank you for teaching me about God.
Thank you for your wisdom and ingenuity.
I miss your laughter and sage advice.
Thank you for teaching me how to be tenacious and faithful.
Because of you, I know the power of prayer and obedience.
Rest in power, Queen.

Robbie L. Jackson (Ivory)
Living Matriarch: Mother

* * * * * * * *

Dear Mama,
I love you and I appreciate you.
Thank you for teaching me to be the woman I am today.
Thank you for showing me how to use creativity to thrive.
Thank you for modeling class and integrity.
Thank you for the sacrifices you made and the love you give.
Because of you, I know how to rise from the ashes.
I will be your strength and support until
you take your last breath.

Bobbie Lee Pullian (Ivory)
Maternal Matriarch: Aunt
Ancestor since 1980

* * * * * * * *

Dear Auntie,
I love you. I miss you. Thank you for loving me fiercely.
Thank you for your fire and fearlessness.
Thank you for modeling what it means to be unapologetic.
Thank you for teaching me how to pay the cost to be the boss.
Thank you for the joy and laughter.
Because of you, I move through the
world unbossed and unbothered.
Rest in power, Queen.

PROLOGUE

I can't breathe.

I can't breathe.

I can't breathe!

Too loud.

Too dark.

Too light.

Too bossy.

I can't breathe.

Too independent.

Too ratchet.

Too bougie.

Too ghetto.

I can't breathe.

No, you can't touch my hair.

No, I ain't your mammy.

No, I won't be your footstool.

Damn, I can't breathe.

I can't breathe.

Too strong.

Too bold.

I'm tired.

I can't breathe.

Stop touching me.

Leave me alone.

No, I don't want to explain.

What the hell you looking at?

I can't breathe.

Can I just live?

White toxicity consuming all the space.

Get out of my way.

Damn, can I get a seat at the table?

Ain't I a woman?

Get off my neck!

I can't f*cking breathe!

I'm dying…

Yes, it's my real hair!

Get your hands off my mouth.

Stop silencing me.

I'm tired.

I can't breathe.

Yes, I'm angry.

Sick of folks pressuring me.

Do you hear me screaming?

No, I won't move out the way.

I don't owe you a smile.

I don't owe you shit!

Did you hear me say I can't breathe!

I'm tired of being woke.

Why are you staring at me?

I'm falling, y'all!

Do you hear me?

Do you see me?

I said I can't breathe!

I don't owe you nothing.

I'm not your negro!

I'm tired of shucking and jiving!

Whew...

I can't catch my breath.

I'm losing it.

So tired.

Stop touching my children.

What'd you say to me?

Watch my tone?

Damn.

Can I catch my breath?

I can't breathe. I can't freaking breathe!

I'm dying.

Can you see my pain?

No, I won't teach you.

I'm not a resource.

Can I just have some joy?

No, I won't wait my turn!

No, I won't shrink.

I'm drowning, y'all.

I'm tired.

You too, Sis?

You causing me pain, too?

Not you too, Black Woman.

It hurts!

Damn.

Ain't no safe place for black women.

It's too much.

I can't take it.

Sick of shifting and shuffling.

My feet hurt.

I'm exhausted.

I can't breathe!

Damn, another black person killed?

Stop killing us!

Does anybody care?

Who is going to protect us?

Stop bumping into me.

I do not have to concede.

No, I don't work here!

Why are you following me?

Do you see my tears?

I'm weak.

I'm overwhelmed!

Somebody help me!

Please!

Whew...

Whew...

I'm suffocating.

Gasp...

Silence...

Wait, Sis!

Keep breathing.

Don't you quit.

Don't you give up.

I got you.

Get up, Sis.

You are not alone.

I know your pain.

Your rage is justified.

Here, have some of my breath.

My strength.

Lean on me.

I got you.

Get up.

You can make it through this.

Let me carry you for a while.

I see you. I hear you.

Don't let them kill you!

Puff...

Puff...

Puff...

Sis.

Inhale.

Breathe.

C'mon, Sister.

You are a Queen.

Do you know who you are?

Puff...

Puff...

Puff...

You are valuable.

You matter.

I love you.

I need you.

You need you.

We need you.

C'mon, Sis.

I love you, Sis.

Don't give up.

There is royalty in your blood.

You got dreams to fulfill.

Breathe!

Breathe!

Breathe!

Your destiny is waiting for you.

You don't have to do it alone.

I know you're tired.

It's okay to be vulnerable.

I got you.

Puff...

Puff...

Puff...

Gasp...

Whew!

Whew!

Inhale...

Exhale...

You're breathing!

Inhale.

Open your eyes, Sis!

You can breathe.

Take a deep breath.

Hold on to me.

I got you.

Stand up.

Stand on the shoulders of your ancestors!

They are with you.

I am with you.

Breathe.

Breathe, Sis!

Rise up.

Rise up!

Yes!

That's right. You can do this!

Rise up, Sis!

From those ashes...

Don't let the fire consume you!

Yes, you're standing up!

Hold your head up.

Breathe!

Rise up!

Rise.

Up.

* * * * * * *

I don't know what kind of ashes you may be standing
in right now.

I don't know the pain you might be experiencing.

I don't know your struggles and fears.

I don't know what you're going through.

But I do know this: you don't have to go through it alone.

I know you're valuable and that you matter.

I know what the fire feels like.

I've been through storms, too.

I know your rage is justified.

I know that the fire can consume you if you let it.

I know that you can rise from your ashes.

I know that you can become the fire.

I will go through the storm with you.

I will rage with you. I will become the fire with you.

I'm here with and for you.

I got you.

It's time to rise up, Sis!

Rise up and go on this journey into the dimensions of

Unf*ckablewith with me.

It's time.

It's time to rise up into your Black Woman Badassery!

Let's go!

INTRODUCTION

UNF*CKABLEWITH

Catriceology: *Slang. Badass Black Woman Resiliency.*

Adjective: *The unbothered and unapologetic ability to rise from the ashes into Black Woman Badassery. The activation of Black Girl Magic to resist, rise, revolutionize, and thrive.*

Unf*ckablewith is a love letter to black women. It's for you, Black Woman. It's balm for your soul, salve for your wounds, light in your darkness, and fire for your belly. It's poetic justice.

Unf*ckablewith is a stiff drink when you've had enough. It's wind for your wings. It may even make you smile or release a healing belly laugh. It's an opportunity to heal your spirit.

Unf*ckablewith is a mirror of affirmation. It's a soul hug. It's a call for you to step into your unique power. It's a tribute to all black women: past, present, and future. It's ignition for your fire.

This book is all of these things, and it's just for you. Because Malcolm X wasn't lying when he said, "The most disrespected person in America is the black woman. The most unprotected person in America is the black woman. The most neglected person in America is the black woman." I'd like to update his statement with "black women everywhere." Malcolm uttered those infamous words in 1962, but not much has changed for us since then. It's way past time for a change. One thing is for sure, black women cannot sit around waiting for respect. You must claim it, reclaim it, and relentlessly obtain it.

In *Unf*ckablewith*, I pay homage to three extraordinary and brave black women. Three magical matriarchs in my family who've shown me the way out of no way through their beautiful struggle called life. By highlighting the struggles in their lives, I mine for the gold and share it with you to affirm that there is light in all dark moments. And that you, too, can make it through and do more than survive. You can thrive!

Through my sharing of these truth-inspired stories and my personal experiences, my hope is that you learn you are not alone in the storms you may be facing. Throughout the book, I also recognize and celebrate the Black Woman Badassery of ten black women heroines who have paved—and continue to pave—the way for black women's freedom, justice, liberation, and healing. My wish for you is that you will say yes to becoming a black woman heroine by leaving your authentic flavor of *Unf*ckablewith* legacy behind for future generations to feast on and metabolize as fuel for their fire.

At the end of each chapter, I offer tips, prompts, and space for self-exploration and personal reflection to help you uproot, embrace, and ignite your own personal *Unf*ckablewith* revolution. My intention for this self-help personal memoir is to remind you of your melanin magic. Yes, Sis, you too have Black Girl Magic, and you can use it to relentlessly rise from your ashes into your own version of Black Woman Badassery to thrive on your own terms.

My ultimate hope as you embark on a journey into new healing dimensions is that you will unleash your *Unf*ckablewith* and be unwavering about who you are. That you will be unapologetic about your blackness and that you'll be unbothered by the storms and fire that try to consume you. I hope you blaze up and become the fire to thrive in your magnificence! Are you ready to say, "damn the white gaze" and rise up into your Black Woman Badassery? Let this love letter to you be the fierce and loving wind beneath your black wings!

CATRICE M. JACKSON

UNF*CKABLEWITH

Catriceology: Slang. Badass Black Woman Resiliency.

Adjective: The unbothered and unapologetic ability to rise from the ashes into Black Woman Badassery. The activation of Black Girl Magic to resist, rise, revolutionize, and thrive.

CATRICE M. JACKSON

"DO NOT LET THE FIRE BURN YOU. BECOME THE FIRE AND BLAZE UP. ACTIVATE YOUR BLACK GIRL MAGIC. RISE. THRIVE. SHINE."

CATRICE M. JACKSON

HARRIET TUBMAN

TENACIOUS

"I would fight for my liberty so long as my strength lasted, and if the time came for me to go, the Lord would let them take me."

Harriet Tubman

* * * * * * *

CHAPTER ONE

TENACIOUS

Ain't this some shit! What the heck is going on up in here? That's what my thirteen-year-old brain was thinking, but I knew damned well not to say it out loud. I thought back to the time when my mother had made a promise to me. Her words had thundered clearly in my mind and echoed for what seemed like forever. I'd never forget those words, because they were powerful and comforting. They were my security blanket. My mama, she was all I had to keep me safe. Safe from pedophiles and men who could molest me. Safe from the dangers of the world. She was a single parent, my life and joy depended on trusting her, and I did. But when the time came, in this moment, I wasn't quite sure I trusted her as much as I thought I did. Yet I knew I desperately *needed* to believe my mama!

Stumbling in the dark, eyes half-closed, I saw him sitting on the couch and thought, *Who are you and what the hell are you doing here?* Maybe I was dreaming. I sure couldn't believe what I was seeing. But yes, as I returned to my bedroom after using the bathroom, there he sat, like he was *supposed* to be there. Had my mama lost her mind? How dare she bring him into our home! The audacity of him sitting on the couch like it was a normal occurrence! I was pissed. A tear rolled down my face as I lay in the dark feeling scared and betrayed. That single tear turned into a silent stream of cries. I was shocked and confused, but mostly I felt anger toward my mother. I tossed and turned. I cried. But eventually I fell asleep with one clear thought in mind: *He better not be here in the morning!*

The next day, I couldn't get out of bed fast enough to see if *he* was still there. He was. I stomped back to my room and pouted like a six-year-old. I felt exposed, discombobulated, and unprotected. I didn't know what to do, but one thing was for sure: I was angry! You see, back then I didn't know who my daddy was. I wasn't used to a man being in our home, and I sure as hell wasn't used to no man telling me what to do. It had been me, my mother, and my older brother in our home from day one. Today I understand that buried underneath my seething anger was sadness, fear, and some jealousy. Today I understand that mama needed someone to love her too. But then, back when I was thirteen, he who sat on my couch was interrupting our lives. He who sat on my couch was taking up my and my brother's space. He who sat on my couch made me feel unsafe.

I didn't feel unsafe because this man said or did anything inappropriate. I felt unsafe because I had been told stories of what some men do to little girls. I felt unsafe because I didn't know how to exist in a living space with a man present. I felt unsafe because of the unknown. I didn't know what to expect, and I didn't know how to protect myself if it became necessary. Deep down in my heart, I just knew I needed to believe the words my mother had spoken to me a few years earlier. I don't remember the complete conversation or why it was initiated. But I'll always remember my mother saying, "I'll never bring a man into our home permanently until you are old enough to confront him and defend yourself."

Back when my mother spoke those unforgettable words to me, I hadn't truly understood what she meant until I saw this man taking up space that didn't belong to him. But intuitively, I had known the gravity and severity of her words. Now, for the first time in my life, I felt exactly what she had meant about being at an age where I could protect myself, because I sure was feeling defensive. I had no idea what could happen next. I sat in my bedroom with the door open, conjuring up my action plan and still freaking pissed that he was here! Scenario after scenario played in my mind:

Who is this man and where did he come from?

How did my mama find him?

What will I do if he says something to me that I don't like?

How will I confront him?

How will I protect myself?

What if he tries to hurt my mama?

Next thing I knew, this dude came out of my mother's bedroom and moved through the house like he'd been there before. As he walked by my bedroom door to go sit on the couch, he said, "Hey, how are you doing?" I said, "I'm all right," while giving him a seriously suspicious side eye. It was awkward. He was uncomfortable. I was uncomfortable. Neither of us knew what to say next. So we said nothing. I sat in my room looking into the living room as he sat on the couch looking at the television. I made my way into the living room and sat at the table. He and I sat in silence until my mother came in. And then we all made superficial small talk to ease the glaring discomfort. My mother broke the silence and officially introduced him to me as her "friend." She said his name was Andrew. He said, "You can call me Stone, that's my nickname." *Stone?* I thought. *Nah! I'll call him Andrew if I must call him at all.*

Yes, I was salty about my mother's new "friend." She wasn't the type of woman who brought men to the house, so I knew this was serious or heading that way. And if I'm honest with myself today, that was part of my fear back then. Fear that it wouldn't just be us anymore, and that my brother and I would have to share our mother with someone else after having her to ourselves all these years. I wasn't sure whether I was old enough to defend myself, as my mother would say, but I was damn sure ready to try if needed. Deep down in my soul, I knew Andrew was here to stay. He was, and he did.

* * * * * * *

Not only did Andrew stay, he became my stepfather. Today I can genuinely say that I loved Andrew. But I didn't love all the things I watched my mama go through in three-plus bittersweet decades of marriage. As the years passed by, I began to understand why he called himself Stone and why my mother waited so long to get married. Andrew was what some might call a cool cat. He loved to style and profile in his Stetson hats and Stacy Adams shoes, and he was definitely the life of the party. Hell, often he was the party! He was a small-built, tough-acting kind of guy. Always puffing up his bird chest, as my mother called it. He talked a good game and tried to be hard, yet there was a softer version of him who showed up at times.

A softer version my mother didn't really know how to receive. She had difficulty showing physical affection in general, but with Andrew, she seemed to struggle more. My mother was a homebody. A five foot three, darker-skinned, full-figured, beautiful homebody. She was classy but not flashy. But when my mama got dressed up to go somewhere special, she always looked phenomenal! Still, she didn't go out to clubs often or run the streets, as they say. I don't think I've ever seen my mother be the life of a party. Unlike Andrew, she was laid back and found honor in being a housewife and mother. How she and Andrew hooked up is still a great mystery. I guess it's true that opposites attract, because my mama was nothing like her husband. Nothing. Andrew was one tough cookie. His nickname Stone fit him perfectly.

My mother was what you might call a "good girl." She was poised, polished, and articulate. She always strived for her version of perfection, and she raised us to be well-mannered, upstanding human beings. She was a woman of great integrity, and she enjoyed caring for her family and capitalizing on her natural gifts of sewing, designing, and art. I would call her an artist. She drew and painted the most beautiful expressions of black women I had ever seen, and for several years she designed her own clothing and hosted fashion shows in our community. Her designs were one-of-a-kind whimsical badass masterpieces. *Sparkle Fashions* was the name of her clothing line, and man, did people shine when they wore her creations. There was no one in our community who could design clothes like my mama. She was quiet and reserved, but she had no problem standing her ground. She said what she meant, and she meant what she said. She was *Unf*ckablewith*! She was steady, constant, and dependable. My brother and I knew we could always count on our mama! This was affirming to me.

My mother was one of six children and the oldest daughter

raised in a home with parents (my grandparents) who seemed to live in the realm of extremes. By "extremes," I mean there seemed to be no middle ground, no neutral. Instead, the energy of my grandparents' personalities and home environment was black or white, right or wrong, good or bad. I didn't realize this as a child, but the distinction is very clear to me today. I also don't remember witnessing a lot of laughter and joy between my grandparents. It was rare to see them hug, touch, or express affection toward one another. Yet I sensed they loved each other. My grandfather, we called him Poppy, was grouchy and stubborn, but when my Gran wanted something, he made sure she got it. After a lot of bitching and moaning, of course. I remember on rare occasions my Gran would plop herself on his lap and he'd act like he was bothered, but he'd smile, and he sure didn't tell her to get up. It was a weird kind of love, but love nonetheless. Like Andrew and my mama, my grandparents were quite the opposite of each other.

My grandfather grew up in the Great Depression of the 1930s, and just about everything about him was reminiscent of that time of struggle, lack, and scarcity. Poppy was beyond frugal; he was downright stingy. The kind of stingy where he'd lick his fingers to check five or six times to see if he was giving you just one dollar while complaining about giving it the whole time. He was so stingy that if he sent me to the grocery store to get something that cost ninety-nine cents, he wanted his penny when I got back. And if I didn't bring it along with a receipt, I heard about it for weeks. Getting anything from him was always a struggle, and that included conversation.

I remember my grandmother having to ask my grandfather to unlock the cupboards and the deep freezer so she could get out food to cook for dinner. She used to get so upset, and they would argue every single time she asked. And he moved at a snail's pace while griping and complaining with every slow and resentful step. The only times I recall not witnessing this extreme ritual was when my grandfather wanted to cook. Then he'd get the ingredients out himself. Seriously, who locks up food? My grandfather, a product of the Great Depression's callous conditioning of scarcity, that's who. Locks, locks, and more locks. There were locks on just about everything in my grandparents' house, including their bedroom door. I don't know how my Gran endured this way of life, but she did, until Poppy took his last breath. This is how she chose to be tenacious.

Because my mother grew up in her parents' house of extremes, I believe she navigated the world through a black-and-white lens that was both affirming and detrimental. One thing I will say, she worked hard to not pass on the extremes to us, but a few slipped past her. I love her dearly, yet growing up in her house there were strict rules that my brother and I were expected to follow, especially when it came to doing chores. During my childhood, there was a right way and a wrong way to do things, according to my mother, and I was careful to do them right as often as possible. Partly because I wanted to make her happy, but mostly because I didn't want to get in trouble.

Listen. My mama didn't play around when it came to keeping a clean and orderly house. As she would say, it needed to be spotless, and if it wasn't, it was not right in her eyes. We were expected to make our beds before we left for school. As soon as we came home, the first expectation was to take off our school clothes that she worked so hard to provide and to put on play clothes. The next expectation was to get busy doing our chores, which ranged from washing dishes to taking out the trash and everything in between. Up until Andrew showed up, she was a single mother raising two biological kids by herself and a nephew she raised since he was a one-year-old baby. And even after Andrew's arrival, my mama was in charge. There was no doubt about it. Mama "wore the pants," and although he knew it, you couldn't tell him he was not THE man. And every chance he got, he reminded her. That used to tickle the hell out of me because I knew my mama was the boss! And so did he.

My mother had been disabled due to a work injury to her back for as long as I can remember. In fact, I don't recall her ever working outside the home. As a result, homemaking was her full-time job, and she took it seriously. Seriously. There was a right and wrong way to fold towels, a right and wrong way to wash the dishes, a right and wrong way to make a bed. When I didn't fold the towels the way she wanted, she would unfold them and show me how to do it "right." And guess what, I still fold my towels the same way today! She would do the same thing with the bed and the dishes: make us start over and do it the correct way. And let's keep it real here. The expectations were even greater for me, because I was the girl. Isn't that how it goes? We raise our daughters and spoil our sons. Yeah, my brother seemed to get more lenience than I did, although my mom would disagree. These are just a few examples of how the extremes I talked about earlier showed up in my mother's way of being.

Andrew was loud and gregarious, while my mother was soft-spoken and low-key. Andrew was "junky" (according to my mother), and my mother was extremely tidy. He was outgoing, she was more introverted. Andrew loved to socialize, and my mother didn't crave the social life like he did unless it was an event she was putting on. He could go from zero to one hundred when he was angry, and she was slow to anger unless the right button was pushed. Andrew was affectionate, and my mother was not into public displays of affection. So yes, opposites apparently do attract. Like my grandparents, my mother and stepfather didn't seem to have much in common, but they loved each other.

As with any marriage, my mother's had its ups and downs. I can make the same observation about my mother's marriage that I did of my grandparents' marriage: they were two people living and loving in the extremes. And although my mother and grandmother endured and were tenacious, I believe they both longed for more gray moments in their marriages. By "gray," I mean a space of peace without extremes, a space of loving on each other without conflict, a space of truly enjoying each other's company, and a space of being content and fulfilled with what they had. But it seems like they didn't know how to consistently move toward finding and cultivating common ground with their husbands. And when they did, it was a rare delight to witness.

Or maybe my mother and grandmother were afraid to be soft and vulnerable. Because black women aren't often taught how to say yes or be open to love, how to be "submissive," or how to show their weaknesses. Whatever you call that space of "not always having to be strong," it isn't something we are often taught. My mother didn't teach me this way of being, so I had to make a conscious effort to learn it on my own. I'm still learning by trial and error, and it often feels foreign to me. Yet I know I need and deserve this softness and vulnerability to truly experience all the sweet moments of life. There is both a spoken and unspoken rule that says black women must always be strong. Collectively, black women are expected to endure by any means necessary through the extremes of life. Expected to be tenacious no matter the cost (and I've learned that tenacity is both a blessing and a curse). To persist even when they feel like passing out. To take more. To do more. To be more for everyone else but themselves.

My grandmother endured. My mother endured. They were tenacious about being committed to their marriages by any means necessary, it seems. I used to be critical of their choices and judged them for choosing to weather their storms the way they did. Now I understand that staying married as a black woman despite the struggles was the expectation and the norm during their generations (and maybe even today). Against all odds and through this bittersweet rite of passage, black women are often encouraged and applauded for their unyielding tenacity, endurance, stamina, persistence, and tirelessness.

Time after time, black women are expected to rise from the ashes of pain, suffering, heartbreak, and oppression. They are expected to scoop those hot ashes up and magically transform them into something useful. Screw making lemonade out of lemons! Black women are expected to create a five-star, four-course meal out of one damn lemon. Damn that lemonade! We are expected to take those sour-ass lemons and create a smorgasbord of lemon-flavored delectables at the drop of a dime. And we are expected to do this endlessly, without complaining.

No matter what life served to my mother and grandmother, they weathered the storms. They survived. They persevered. Throughout my life I've seen my mother and grandmother bend, but never break. I've seen their emotional capacity stretched to the point of exhaustion, and then watched them bounce back like champs. They've fallen and gotten back up. They made a way out of no way. These black women, my mother and grandmother, seemed to be emotionally infallible and spiritually grounded. They believed that if God brought them to it, that He'd also take them through it. And He did, because their faith muscles were strong. I never understood the power and suffering of having enormous emotional resiliency until I got married.

I too have weathered many storms within my marriage. Because my mother wasn't good at modeling affection between a man and woman, I didn't have any reference. I saw how my grandparents engaged and knew I didn't want that kind of love. And because for the first twelve years of my life there was no man (father) in the home, I didn't experience healthy, affectionate relationships with men. This was something I knew I would have to teach myself. I didn't have the skills, so I prayed for a man who was highly affectionate. And thank God, my husband is. But I still had to teach myself how to receive it. Having my son was my greatest teacher. My affection for him was constant, enduring, and unconditional. And if I'm honest, my husband has also been a great teacher on a soul level. Through my marriage and being willing to be loved, soft, and vulnerable, I believe I have broken that generational curse.

Like most couples, we've argued, disagreed, and hurt each other out of our own fears and insecurities. We've forgiven each other and worked through the storms. Sometimes barely. There were times I wanted to quit and walk away. There was a time I signed the papers and then changed my mind. There were times when we were apart and took breaks from one another. Yet our souls knew we were meant for each other. Two people committed to love and marriage, but we are opposites too. Isn't that hilarious!

Much like my mother, I am a neat freak and love cleanliness and order. And much like Andrew, my husband has the tendency to be junky. He's athletic. I hate exercise. He's not much of a talker, and my voice chakra is wide open. Those are just a few ways we are different. And even though we get frustrated and angry, we are still here. Still together, weathering the stormy realities and truths of marriage. Tenaciously making it through. And in full transparency, I've often looked back on the marriages of my grandmother and mother, and I can see how engrained generational behaviors are.

I've also said, "Geez! I'm just like my mother and grandmother in some ways." I guess I can say that love and commitment require mining for gold every day; that's how you keep finding and being reminded of the glitter and shine that you saw when you first got married. It takes a special kind of man to deal with an *Unf*ckablewith* wife. And my husband is special.

Yes. My mother and grandmother were dedicated, tenacious, and unyielding warrior queens. And they were also *Unf*uckablewith*! If I had to assign a motto for how they lived in relation to men (and anyone else, for that matter), it would be, "Don't start nothing and it won't be nothing." I come from a line of strong black women who didn't take no shit from anyone, especially any man. My mama was *Unf*ckablewith* in so many splendid ways. My mama would bring someone their hat (call you on your shit when necessary), as the older women in my family used to say. She didn't bother anyone, and she kept to herself, but if the right button was pushed, she too could go from zero to one hundred. When it came to her children, she was *Unf*ckablewith*. Sounds like me! Yeah, that's totally me.

When it came to my mama's craft as a genius artist and clothing designer, she was *Unf*ckablewith*. I'm talking about an MC Hammer, can't-touch-this type of *Unf*ckablewith*. She was a master at the extreme of perfectionism, and when she used her hands to create, she was in a league of her own. Even during periods of scratching and surviving, my mama was nobody's fool, and she didn't take no wooden nickels. In other words, she didn't let other people fool her or take advantage of her. Strong, resilient, steadfast, and enduring. My mother and grandmother were two women who mostly talked softly but carried big sticks. They were *Unf*ckablewith*!

Now that I'm married, I have a better understanding about why they weathered and endured. Like my mother and grandmother, I took my vows seriously, and if possible, I plan on being married until death do us part. When I was younger, I thought it was ridiculous that they put up with so much. Wiser, more mature, and married almost twenty years myself, it makes sense. I get it. Marriage. It's bitter and sweet and takes a lot of effort to make it work. I don't judge them anymore. Instead, I mine for the gold in the lessons of their lives and use it to add some sparkle to my life and marriage. I value their lessons now more than I ever did before.

It's important for me to make this point as well: while my mother and grandmother chose to be tenacious in their commitments to their marriages, that is not the expected choice for all black women. I encourage you to craft your own unique relationship with your partner. Some choices are healthier than others, but there is no right or wrong choice, just your choice. This applies not only to intimate relationships, but also to friendships. By sharing these stories of tenacity, I'm choosing to honor the resiliency of my elders and to celebrate their capacity and will to survive and thrive in the best ways they knew how. But I'm also keenly aware that my mother's and grandmother's choices to weather their storms were byproducts of intergenerational trauma and black family cultural traditions (often expectations).

I haven't done any formal studies or conducted any empirical research on this, but the fact that my great-grandmother was oppressed and tenaciously endured, that my grandmother was oppressed and tenaciously endured, that my mother was oppressed and tenaciously endured, leads me to believe that I too am oppressed and tenaciously endure. The pain of and response to oppression is a trauma my ancestors experienced several generations ago, and it was planted in and passed on to their descendants in the womb. This trauma has been transmitted to each generation as a means of literal and social survival, and the ensuing thought processes and behaviors then become the default or norm within "black culture." This is *oppression retention*. This is what generational curses look like in real time. Some might argue this is also what dysfunction looks like in real life. The wounds of oppression run deep. And each generation is responsible for doing their part to heal these soul wounds, so that we eventually rid ourselves of this legacy of trauma and oppression.

I find truth in this, because I know through generational storytelling and observation of the behaviors of my mother and grandmother that I am less "dysfunctional" than the generations before me. My mother didn't put up with or choose to tolerate certain things my grandmother did. After observing my mother's life and marriage, there are things she put up with or chose to tolerate that I don't. And although I have only one child, a son, I am teaching him to not put up with or tolerate what I chose to (or had to) endure in my life and marriage. I am relentlessly committed to breaking generational curses and shattering the chains of oppression.

I believe this is one way that we can help facilitate black liberation. As each generation of black folks commits to its soul healing, we will see less trauma in our descendants. Eventually, we will stop retaining and transmitting the trauma response. I believe our healing must include learning the truth about our ancestors before they were colonized and brutalized. I believe it must include detoxifying ourselves from the ravenous infection of whiteness. I believe it must include reclaiming ancestral traditions and practices that cultivate healing and community. And I believe it must include becoming conscious and waking up our children and future generations to the power in being black, whole, healed, free, and liberated.

This soul work. This trauma healing, especially for black women, is not only possible but critical to our health and well-being. It's essential for the healing of black women's wounds and *thrival* of blackness. It's necessary for us to experience deep wholeness and joy. When we black women do our personal work to heal our trauma pain, we pass on a less-oppressed life to our children. We can then teach our sons, daughters, nieces, nephews, and grandchildren to be free of pain and exist in wholeness despite oppressive systems. When black women recognize that our bittersweet traits of tenacity, perseverance, and resiliency can also be trauma responses to oppressive pain, then we are equipped with the powerful knowledge that surrender, vulnerability, and compassion for ourselves can serve as tools for healing, transformation, and freedom. These are priceless and life-saving tools to defy and transcend the storm.

You may not be weathering the same storms as my mother and grandmother. But we all have storms we are weathering. What is your storm? What are you struggling with? You may not be enduring what they've endured, but you're enduring something you're ready to move on from. What are you putting up with? Who are you tolerating? How are you settling? I want you to know that you too are *Unf*ckablewith*! If you feel like you're burning with doubt, misery, pain, and struggle, know instead that you are on fire, a phoenix who embodies melanin magic that empowers you to rise from the ashes into your full Black Woman Badassery. You can choose tenacity. If there is one time to be tenacious, it is now. Be tenacious about your healing. You can choose surrender and vulnerability. You can choose whatever you want to choose. Don't let the fire consume you. Instead, become the fire, blaze up, and activate your black girl magic to rise, thrive, revolutionize, and shine!

Writing Prompts to Rise from the Ashes

What storms are you weathering?

_____

_____

_____

_____

_____

_____

_____

_____

How do your resiliency and tenacity show up?

_____

_____

_____

_____

_____

_____

_____

_____

What ashes are you sitting in that you want to rise above?

_____

_____

_____

_____

_____

_____

_____

What generational trauma is still present in your life?

_____

_____

_____

_____

_____

_____

What do you need to heal?

_____

_____

_____

_____

_____

_____

_____

How will you embody your melanin magic?

_____

_____

_____

_____

_____

_____

_____

_____

_____

_____

How will you be tenacious about your healing?

_____

_____

_____

_____

_____

_____

_____

_____

_____

_____

SHIRLEY CHISHOLM

UNBOSSED

"We must reject not only the stereotypes that others hold of us, but also the stereotypes that we hold of ourselves."

Shirley Chisholm

* * * * * * *

CHAPTER TWO

UNBOSSED

I could hear my family moving around in the other rooms of my grandmother's house. There were sudden bursts of robust laughter, and it seemed like every light in the house was on except for the one in the den, where I was cuddled up with my little cousin Corey in the top bunk. It was the night before Christmas. I was eleven years old and Corey was going to turn one the day after Christmas. It wasn't uncommon for me to be lugging around and caring for a baby. That's how I got my nickname Nan. My family started calling me Nanny because of my love for babies and my natural caretaker instincts, and as I got older, Nanny was shortened to Nan.

My little cousin and I were supposed to be sleeping so we could wake up in the morning to see what Santa Claus had brought us. Corey didn't want to go to sleep, and I was being nosy, trying to see what the grownups were doing and talking about. Every now and then I would sit up in the bed and peek into the dining room to see what was going on. For some reason, other than the typical night-before-Christmas excitement, I felt compelled to stay up until my aunt, my only and favorite Aunt Bobbie, arrived. She was Corey's mother and they would be celebrating their first Christmas together along with his older sister, Nicole, who was also there. Aunt Bobbie loved Christmas, and I loved everything about her. She was like a second mother to me and we spent a lot of time together. We were all waiting for her to show up.

My Aunt Bobbie was everything! And she was *Unf*ckablewith*! She was gregarious, sassy, hilarious, and fun-loving, but those words describe only a tiny bit of her gloriousness. Even though I was young, I sensed that men loved my Aunt Bobbie. She was beautiful! She commanded the attention of men wherever she went simply by showing up. Their attraction to her was undeniable. Back when I was a kid, I wouldn't have thought to use the word "sexy" to describe her, but that's what she was: alluring, magnetic, and mesmerizing. She was always styling and profiling while rocking my mom's unique outfits made just for her. Her nickname was Pudding—my mother called her Pudd—and I imagine she earned it because she was very sweet. I really don't know how her nickname came about, but when Pudding walked into the room, all the men paused. What I knew back then was that when we were with her, we all felt alive.

Pudding was my mom's only sister, her baby sister, and they loved each other so much. I remember them always being together, so much so that we often lived close to her. My mother used to say I acted more like my aunt than I did her. My auntie had no problem calling a thing a thing, speaking her truth, and telling folks off if she needed to, and she did it without batting an eye. Vicariously I learned the art of sass from her and my grandmother. Like the old folks say, "We were cut from the same cloth." No one bossed my aunt around. She was the boss of herself and the men she dated knew they were just along for the ride, just living in her world. Her nieces and nephews knew she was the boss. Hell, her siblings knew not to mess with Pudding, or else!

When I would stay the night at her house, she was fun yet firm. She allowed us to play, laugh, and have a good time, but we knew when she meant business and when it was time to sit our asses down somewhere! Either way, I stayed with her every chance I could get. She would tell the funniest jokes, play games with us, and she loved to laugh. One of our favorite games was charades. Aunt Bobbie was serious about charades, okay! She totally embodied what she was acting out with hilarious facial expressions and hand gestures; she killed it every time. I would roll on the floor laughing deep belly laughs until my stomach hurt and I could barely breathe. She was funny as hell! I think her sense of humor was magnetic too. People loved to be around her because she believed in having a good time no matter what life challenges she was facing.

My aunt was feisty. She said whatever the hell she wanted and gave zero f*cks about what other people thought about her. The word "unbothered" doesn't even begin to describe how she moved through the world. She was the epitome of unbossed before I even knew what it meant. She was in charge of her life, even to her detriment. She was always talking about "paying the cost to be the boss." I didn't understand what she meant at the time, but now I know she meant that if you're going to be the boss of your life, you need to be ready to pay for the risks you take and the choices you make. She meant that if you want something, then boss up and make it happen. She meant that sometimes you'll lose in order to win. And sometimes, losses will be more than you can handle, and you simply roll with the punches in life.

It seems like my aunt was in a perpetual cycle of rolling with the punches. Alcoholism was kicking her ass. She was never able to win that battle. At one point in her life, she suffered a stroke that contorted one side of her face, but it didn't stop her from living her life on her own terms. Good, bad, or indifferent, she made her own choices and dealt with the consequences, no matter what they were. She loved to drink, and it was rare to see her not drinking or drunk. I didn't realize how often she drank until I was old enough to truly understand what excessive drinking and alcoholism were. Today, I realize my favorite aunt would often drink to numb the pain of whatever haunted her sober mind. I don't know everything that happened to Aunt Bobbie as a child and young woman, but she appeared to have found ways to escape that both harmed her and brought her comfort and joy.

I imagine growing up in my grandparents' house of extremes played a part in her pain. And possibly it was irreconcilable pain. From the stories my mother told me, it seems like there wasn't much room for her and her siblings to error. According to my mother, Pudding experienced some treacherous childhood trauma that she didn't fully recover from. Despite her pain, my aunt loved her son and daughter and was absolutely smitten with them. And despite her inner struggles, my aunt was a boss! A damn boss, ya hear me! She didn't take no shit, she was brutally honest, and when it came to her family, she loved us fiercely. My aunt didn't allow other people to order her around. She was a self-governed woman and not to be messed with.

So back to the night before Christmas. Finally, Corey fell asleep, and I realized it was well after midnight. The lights were still on, but there was an eerie silence in the house. Something wasn't right. I could sense it. I was too young to know what intuition was, but I felt a deep sense of emptiness and fear. Instinctively, I hugged Corey tighter, as if I knew he could sense the emptiness too. No wonder they named me Nanny: my mother instincts were strong even then.

I didn't know what was happening, but I tried to go to sleep. Right as I was beginning to doze off, I heard a scream that reached down into the most wretched place of human suffering that ever existed. I didn't know who was screaming, but it shook me to the core. I leapt off the top bunk and ran toward the dining room.

"She's gone, oh my God, she's gone!" someone screamed.
Who's gone? I wondered.
"She's gone!" the scream came again. I realized my grandmother and mother were both screaming, over and over.

Somehow, I knew who they meant, but I didn't want to believe it. My aunt, my favorite aunt, my second mama was dead. It was the first time I experienced the death of someone I loved, someone I loved so deeply. I was shocked and devastated. Paralyzed in place, I just stood there watching my mother and grandmother scream and cry. Eventually, I was able to move my body, and I ran back to the den, climbed back into the top bunk, cuddled up tight with Corey, and sobbed and sobbed. So much pain. So much excruciating pain I felt, like nothing I had ever experienced in my life. It was helpless pain, the kind that makes you feel like there is absolutely nothing you can do to stop it. There have been very few moments in my life where I felt like I wanted to or was going to die. This was the first time, and it was also the first time I clearly remember being angry at God for "allowing" this to happen to us.

Much of what happened later that night is a blur. Yet I was wise enough to know that this baby, my little cousin Corey, would never know his imperfect-but-amazing mother. I knew I would have to help my mother raise him and keep him safe. I instantly went into protection mode and began thinking about all the ways I could help. Even at eleven years old. It's what we black girls do. It's what we are directly and vicariously taught to do: to put our pain on the back burner and care for others, even at the expense of our own emotional health. Corey turned one on December 26th of that year, 1980. His mother died on Christmas Eve, and Christmas wasn't the same for us for years to come. In fact, Christmas is still difficult for Corey, and I always remember my auntie at Christmastime. I kept my promise. I helped my mother raise Corey just like he was my little brother, and he is.

How my aunt died is still a mystery. After she didn't show up at my grandparents' house, we sent someone to look for her. Remember, this was before there were cell phones. I don't know all the details of the situation, but I know she was found dead in her own front yard on Christmas Eve. It was alleged that she was drunk and slipped and fell off her front porch, which I remember being about three feet high. I say "alleged" because there were rumors flying around at the time that she had been assaulted based on the wound to her head. I could never understand why someone would try to hurt Pudding; she was sweet to everyone and well-liked, even though she was feisty as hell. To this day, I wonder how long she laid there cold and alone before she was found. She never made it to be with her family, never made it to spend Corey's first Christmas with him.

It was such a sad and breathtaking moment. One that shook me to the core and devastated our family. I felt like I lost a parent too. So much so that I internalized my pain and rage, and it manifested in ways I didn't know how to handle at such a young age. Once a well-behaved child, my sass amplified, and I didn't care about the consequences my smart mouth would bring. I chose to rebel in every way possible. I needed to express my sadness, anger, and unimaginable pain. I really didn't have anywhere to turn. The grown folks in my family were too busy tending to their own wounds and trying to survive. They were trying to be resilient. They didn't have time nor make time to make sure we kids were all right. Plus, a lot of black folks, especially in the late 1970s and early 1980s, did not believe in going to therapy. Hell, I'm not even sure they knew what it was or how to access it. Now that I think about it, neither did I.

As I reflect on that time, I realize I surely could have used some therapy to cope with the grief and anger related to my aunt's death. When she died, a piece of me died too. I was so bitter and verbally combative. I was already sassy as hell, and her death exacerbated my feistiness and fire. I didn't care what I said, how I said it, or who I said it to. Speaking my mind was the only way I had to release the sadness and rage I felt inside. My mama didn't play that, though. She was not the kind of mother who allowed kids to talk back and get smart. And although I was naturally sassy, I knew when to shut my mouth, most times.

Except for one time when I was in the fifth grade, after the events of that Christmas. Like Aunt Bobbie, my mama would say, "You have to pay the cost to be the boss." In other words, I had better be ready to pay or suffer the consequences if I wanted to be the boss and be in charge. My pain was like my aunt's had been—so deep and relentless that I was willing to do whatever the hell I wanted. I thought the consequences would be worth the release. I needed a release. I needed to exhale. I needed to create some kind of control in my life because it felt like my emotions were reckless and running wild. Maybe this was one time in my life when I needed to feel unbossed.

In the early 1980s, black and brown kids were still being bused into predominantly white school districts to create so-called diverse learning communities. I lived on the West Side in Sioux City, Iowa. Now you already know that Iowa is one of the whitest states in the country. And Sioux City was a small and predominantly white city.

Hell, I wouldn't even call it a city. It's more like a town. And for the most part, it was a very segregated city. The West Side, where I grew up, was racially diverse, but still largely white. When I entered the third grade, I was bused to a school on the North Side of town. It sat right on the border, so to speak, between what we'd call the end of the West Side and the beginning of the North Side, which was considered one of the white sections of town. Prior to being bused out of my neighborhood, I went to an elementary school that was much more diverse.

I was generally a well-behaved, average student. For the most part, I got along well with my classmates and teachers. That changed in the fifth grade. I had a mean old white woman as a teacher the year my aunt died. Cranky ole Mrs. Green was the perfect target for releasing my rage. And that's what I did, whenever I could. When I came back to school after Aunt Bobbie died, I simply did not give a damn about anything, especially math, my worst subject. For whatever reason, Mrs. Green kept insisting on picking on me about my incomplete math assignment. She didn't seem to care that I had just experienced a traumatic event and showed no mercy. She didn't show many kids mercy, especially black and brown kids. She was a miserable, stubborn old lady!

That day, Mrs. Green was in an extra pissy mood. She must have had teacher burnout, because she didn't seem to like kids, especially black kids. And we didn't like her, either. She called on me to answer a question about my math assignment. I glared at her and gave no response. She kept calling on me, and I kept refusing to answer while engaging in a staredown with her. Before I knew it, I called her a bitch and told her to leave me alone. In the moment, I didn't care about the consequences of my words. I wanted to be left alone. I wanted to rage on someone. I wanted someone to feel the excruciating pain I felt. I needed to release my pent-up anger and frustration. I didn't know how to ask for help. I sure as hell didn't know how to ask white folks for help. And you know what can happen when black kids tell their business to a white school system. I was smart enough to know that for sure. I made a conscious choice to lash out and didn't care about the repercussions.

And so I paid the cost to be the boss. On that day, I was in charge of my own agency. I made a choice to say something and act in a way that allowed me to release my pain and take care of *my* feelings. Mrs. Green didn't bat an eye. She immediately told me I was out of there and to get out. She escorted me down to the principal's office, and he called my mom to tell her what had happened. I remember sitting in the principal's office scared as hell. Scared of not what the principal would say, but rather of how my mother would respond. Apparently, my behavior was an act of insubordination and warranted either expulsion for a few days or corporal punishment. Hell, my mother was not down for me missing school unless it was absolutely necessary. When the principal got off the phone with her, he informed me that she had given him permission to paddle me. Wow! I still can't believe I received corporal punishment from the principal with my mother's permission. He took me downstairs into the boiler room with no witnesses. Just me, him, and that damn paddle! Yup. I got swatted hard on the behind three times with a wooden paddle and spent the rest of the day in his office!

That paddle was at least an inch and a half thick with four or five cutout circles. I suspect the holes were there to break or cushion the impact. Well, guess what, I was so pissed at everyone—especially my mother—that the impact of the paddle was all I felt while it was happening. *Why did Mom agree to this,* was all I was thinking! And I was sad that no one seemed to care why I was acting out. Can you believe it? When I think about corporal punishment, it blows my mind that it was legal to essentially whip other people's kids. Even worse is that I believe this principal, a black man, enjoyed paddling kids, and he was known for it in the district. I hate to say it, but I also believe he especially enjoyed paddling black kids. As an adult, I now understand that he too was infected with white supremacy, as he had almost no tolerance for black kids. I will never forget that moment. I told you! My mama didn't play around when it came to running your mouth. When I got home from school, I got a good talking to. I have didn't any more problems with Mrs. Green.

* * * * * * *

Unfortunately, sometimes the fire consumes black women and we are not able to continue to rise from the ashes. We stop resisting and surrender to the eye of the storm, and/or we engage in behaviors that intensify the storm to the point of great harm or lethality. Sometimes when the fire tries to consume us, we ingest its toxic chemicals and they dilute and paralyze our power and ability to rise from the ashes. And sometimes the residue from the storm weighs us down and causes us to surrender to the internal and external oppression we experience. We bend. We break. We retreat. We give up. We scratch and fight to survive. And some of us bounce back and rise. Some folks repeat this overwhelming and exhausting cycle their whole lives, while others finally rise out of the ashes into their Black Woman Badassery. They get sick and tired of being sick and tired, and they begin to change the ways they think, behave, and act.

When you rise into your Black Woman Badassery, it doesn't mean you will never experience pain, trauma, or setbacks, it just means you'll choose to push through the pain and not become paralyzed by it. You'll believe you deserve better and do the inner work to heal your pain and soul wounds. It means you will consciously choose to not let the storm consume you. It means that instead of letting the fire burn you, the fire regenerates you. It means you will become the fire! And when you become the fire, you are a force to be reckoned with. You are a badass black woman!

I believe my aunt was both the storm and the victim of the storm. In the short twenty-nine years she was alive, she repeatedly rose from the ashes of her soul wounds. Resisting and persisting through her pain. Being consumed by the fire and becoming the fire. Consciously and unconsciously consuming the toxic residue at the eye of the storm. Scratching and surviving. Rising. Crashing. Burning. Emerging again. Surrendering. And finally, at peace before she rises and rests in her final destination. Free at last, free at last. The cost of freedom can be lethal, which is why I say, *"Live free or die trying."* I can now reflect on my aunt's short life and see exactly how she lived out this cycle of resisting and surrendering to the direct and vicarious traumas she experienced, and how she embodied the spirit of the phoenix. I can clearly recall moments when she was the storm, and moments when the storm consumed her. And even though her surrender was premature, she lived every moment of her life consciously unbossed and unbothered. She literally paid the cost to be the boss!

It makes me wonder just how many of her thoughts, behaviors, and beliefs were due to her environment versus her genetic makeup. How did she learn her survival skills? What caused her maladaptive behaviors? Where did her resiliency come from? What helped her find joy in a life journey tainted with so much struggle and pain? I ask these same questions about my grandmother, my mother, myself, and all the other black women who keep rising from the ashes. In America, black women have crashed, burned, and risen for centuries. And a lot of them are still in this perpetual cycle today. How do we keep surviving and thriving in the eye of the storm? A storm that seems constant and relentless? Hell, black women are fighting to survive multiple storms simultaneously: the tumultuous storms of self, and the societal storms of sabotage and savagery.

What makes black women resist, persist, and rise?

Is there magic in our melanin?

Do we have superpowers?

When are we taught how to scratch, survive, and rise?

Is it in our DNA?

According to epigenetics, the study of biological mechanisms that switch genes on and off, life circumstances can cause certain of your genes to be active or dormant. I heard a great analogy that may help you understand how epigenetics functions. We all come with life scripts (our genes), kind of like movie scripts, for our lives as human beings. However, we each have a unique director (life circumstances and ourselves) who determines things like which scenes to emphasize and which actors to use for each part (genes being switched on and off). To make this clearer, consider this: if the script for the movie *The Color Purple* was directed by Denzel Washington instead of Steven Spielberg, the movie would have played out very differently. Same script, different outcome. This is true for human beings too. Our genes may be very similar (or even identical, in the case of identical twins), but due to unique life circumstances that affect which genes are active or dormant, the experiences and outcomes that occur between our birth and death will be different for each of us.

Epigenetics also suggests that your environment influences your genes; thus behaviors, coping mechanisms, and, as I discussed in Chapter One, even trauma can be transmitted from generation to generation. This can show up in the way you show affection, your beliefs, how you handle stress, the way you parent children, and essentially everything you do. In her book *Post Traumatic Slave Syndrome: America's Legacy of Enduring Injury and Healing*, Dr. Joy DeGruy states that "[t]he legacy of trauma is also passed down through extended family, and community." Many of us are the children and grandchildren of the slave community that endured horrific living conditions. We all carry some form of vicarious trauma, whether it's the result of witnessing trauma within our homes or communities, the result of it being passed down through our genes, or both.

Continuing with the analogy of the movie script, some of us memorize the script and act it out exactly as our mothers did. Some of us create our own adaptation of the script to foster some healing and self-agency. Some of us rewrite the script to create outcomes and experiences different from those of our parents. And some of us toss out the script completely and write our own authentic story. What's probably most common is that we do all of the above at different stages of our lives. When you reflect on the lives of your mother and grandmothers, have you replayed their scripts, created your own adaptation of them, or are you writing a new script unique to the way you want to live your life? It's important to note that not all generational behaviors are negative or unhealthy. I'm sure you can identify behaviors of your mother and grandmothers that you cherish and enact today. Even though my mother and grandmother went through some storms that I did not or chose not to weather, I value the lessons I've learned from their courage and tenacity.

For example, both my mother and grandmother were particular about how they kept their homes. They both were tidy perfectionists and kept their houses spick and span. I appreciate having been taught how to maintain a clean and orderly home. Cleanliness and order are important to me, and sometimes I obsess about how tidy or not my house is. I've learned to relax a little bit in this area of my life, but for me, keeping a clean house is more about creating peace than it is about cleanliness. (In other words, I chose to adapt this particular script to suit my life!) When my home is in order and clean, I experience inner peace, and peace is one of my top five core values. I need it. Especially as a creative person, because I believe it can be difficult to create in chaos. At least I can't. What generational behaviors do you value? Why are they important to you, and are you passing them down to the next generation? At the end of the day, we can choose how we will act out our lives. We can choose what happens in the middle of the script. You can choose to be *Unf*ckablewith*!

The choosing can be hard to do, though. Especially if you grew up in an environment with lots of dysfunction, family chaos, and unhealthy living patterns. If you combine any of that with trauma and/or mental health issues, your cognition and decision-making processes may suffer adverse effects. Mix all of that with your particular personality and temperament, and soon you have a unique storm, one that can result in maladaptive behaviors that can destroy your peace and sabotage your success in life. I speculate this was the recipe my aunt was dealing with. Based on the stories I've heard and the truth I've seen with my own eyes, I conclude this was the script she played out in her life. And while the ending of her script was early and fatal, I also know my aunt loved her family, and she tried her best to experience joy on her own terms. And her terms included remaining unbossed until the end.

We'll never know how the story of my aunt's life could have ended differently, but I'm grateful to have been able to mine the gold from her unbossed existence. When I'm embodying my unbossed-ness, sometimes I smile inside because I know Aunt Bobbie still lives within me. My son has a tattoo on his neck that reads *"Beautiful Struggle."* I was upset when he got it several years ago, but today I understand why he did and what it really means. My aunt's life was a beautiful struggle. Our lives, that's what they are: beautiful struggles. I believe your life is a beautiful struggle too. I'm sure you're ebbing and flowing to navigate life, and sometimes you feel like you are in the eye of the storm. My hope for you is that you recognize the unhealed wounds that may be intensifying your storm and use that knowledge to begin your healing journey. And do it like a boss!

Speaking of a boss! The queen of unbossed is Shirley Chisholm. In 1968, she was the first black woman to be elected to the U.S. Congress, and in 1972, the first black woman to run for President of the United States. She was born in Brooklyn, New York to Barbadian immigrant parents, was sent to live with her grandmother in Barbados at age five, and returned to New York during the Great Depression at age ten. She excelled in predominantly white classrooms and received several scholarships to attend prestigious colleges. Her family could not afford the room and board, however, so Shirley attended Brooklyn College, which is where she got her start in social and political activism.

Shirley became involved in the NAACP and began to speak out for social and racial justice. And she spoke with power and conviction, evolving into a distinguished and deliberate voice for the people. She gained a reputation for calling a thing a thing, and for telling it like it is. She took a stand. And it didn't matter what face she was standing in front of, Shirley challenged the status quo and demanded equality and justice with a vengeance. She was a champion for causes such as the anti-war movement, equal pay, women's rights, and aid for the poor, and she often went to bat for the disenfranchised and marginalized people within her community. She refused to shuck and jive for the white gaze. She was unapologetic as f*ck. Shirley's presidential campaign slogan was "Unbought and Unbossed," and she published a book of the same name in 1970.

Although Shirley didn't win the presidential race, she was nominated as one of the ten most admired women in the world during the peak of her political career. In the face of hatred, racism, and discrimination, she was unbossed. She did things her way, and she didn't give a damn what other people thought of her. She refused to be pimped by the system or controlled by the fear of white folks' opinions. Shirley was unbought. She risked her life and cared little about retaliation from the powers that be. She was committed to being who she was and saying what she damn well pleased. In my opinion, Shirley Chisholm stood in the eye of a racist storm and said, "Aww, hell nah! Y'all ain't gone kill me. Watch me rise up from these ashes and show you just who the f*ck you're dealing with." A strong, unbought, unbossed, badass black woman! Yes, Auntie Shirley, Yesss! Shirley Chisholm took charge of her destiny without asking for permission.

In my book *Unleash Your Significance*, I ask the question, "How will you live out your destiny dash, the space between life and death? You are the screenwriter and the director of your life script. You get to create whatever you want. You may need to cancel some of the actors or add some new ones in. You can choose to change the scenes. You can choose to refuse to play out that old unhealthy generational script. You can mine for the gold and sprinkle it into your new story. You can choose how your stories end." Don't let anyone else write or direct your life story. Take charge and be *Unf*ckablewith.*

Here's a passage from *Unleash Your Significance* that I want you to digest and metabolize as you take back the pen and rewrite your beautiful unbossed story to change what gets passed to the next generations:

THIS IS IT! It's time. Your last beautiful breath is moments away. With every exhale, you feel what you've known as your life becoming a distant memory. This moment, the pinnacle of life as you lived it will be no more in just a few more seconds. Time has run out. There will be no tomorrow. You will never feel the touch of your cherished ones' embrace. You've had your last laugh. Your fears and worries will all be over soon. This is the end of your living journey.

You'll never dance another dance, sing another song, or cry another tear. Faintly, yet distinctly, you hear your name being called. You hear the sweet whisper of your creator's voice lovingly beckoning you to let go to be intimately in his presence. The precious inhale of breath lessens as you linger between the spaces of here and there. This is it. Your time in your beloved body is over! There is no more you and life as you know it. At last... you've taken your last breath.

Have you lived the life you were destined to live? Did you fulfill your purpose? Did you dance with your destiny? Did you really live? Did you take the expensive trip, savor the decadent cake, love unconditionally and fully express the beauty of your soul? Or did you accept what life dished out to you? Were you stingy with your love and affection? Did you guard your wounded heart and never fully experience soulful love? Was your life full of anger, frustration, regret and fear? How much energy did you waste on worrying about what other people thought of you or how much time did you let pass, by fearing failure and being afraid of success?

There are no second chances. This is it! You have one life to live. You were born. And you will die; but how you live in the dash between life and death is up to you, and only you. Are you allowing life to happen to you, or are you creating the moments leading to the fulfillment of your unique destiny?

– Catrice M. Jackson

Be *Unf*ckablewith* and be the boss of your life!

Writing Prompts to Rise from the Ashes

Do you know what your unique soul wounds are?

_____

_____

_____

_____

_____

_____

_____

What are the expectations for black women in your family?

_____

_____

_____

_____

_____

_____

_____

How are you living up to or defying these expectations?

_____

_____

_____

_____

_____

_____

_____

Are you the boss, screenwriter, and director of your life, and if so, how?

_____

_____

_____

_____

_____

_____

_____

What generational scripts will you toss out?

_____

_____

_____

_____

_____

_____

What do you need to heal your trauma?

_____

_____

_____

_____

_____

_____

_____

_____

_____

_____

How do you embody being Unbossed?

_____

_____

_____

_____

_____

_____

_____

_____

_____

_____

"I am sick and tired of being sick and tired."

Fannie Lou Hamer

* * * * * * * *

CHAPTER THREE

RESILIENT

I don't know how many times over my lifetime I've heard my mother say she was sick and tired of being sick and tired. In fact, I recall hearing my Aunt Bobbie say those words too. When I was younger, I wondered what they meant. Now that I am a grown-ass woman, I completely understand what it means to be sick and tired of being sick and tired. Because I've had those days! Damn! Black women, we have some serious resiliency. I mean a kind of resiliency that doesn't seem to exist in any other women like it does in black women. A bittersweet kind of ragged and regal resiliency that both sustains and restrains us. And still, it's that black girl magic kind of resiliency that helps us survive and thrive on our own terms.

A lot of black women have a kind of resilience that can be a barrier to vulnerability, softness, and love. A resiliency so strong it keeps them from getting what they deeply desire and crave. I know black women who desperately want healthy physical affection but are too afraid to give someone a hug or ask for one. An example of how resiliency can be restraining is a person who is unable or unwilling to allow themselves to be in the space of vulnerability required to get their needs met. To get what you want, sometimes you have to ask for it. And if you're too strong and too prideful to ask, your desire goes unfulfilled. I know there are valid reasons why some black women may show up this way, yet their need to be strong doesn't allow for moments of softness to fulfill them. Is your resiliency working against your desires?

Resiliency is how you adapt to trauma, chaos, tragedy, loss, and threats. Resiliency is thoughts, behaviors, and actions that are innate and learned over time that help you navigate daily life stressors. It's your bounce back. It's your come up. It's your grit and hustle. Resiliency is creativity, resourcefulness, and innovation. Resiliency is another desperate inhale when the world is trying to suffocate you. It's waking up every day and entering a world full of land mines and traps designed to kill you. Resiliency is grasping onto your faith when your situation looks bleak. Resiliency is kind of like a rubber band: some stretch farther than others, but they're all breakable. Everyone is resilient, and we all have our breaking points. And sometimes we don't know what our breaking point is until we snap! I often say I'm grateful to have not been alive during chattel slavery or the Jim Crow Era, because I'm not sure I could have weathered those atrocious storms. I can't fathom what some of our ancestors endured during those times.

Some black folks get tired of watching slavery films, but I draw a significant source of wisdom, courage, and strength from them. Of course, those kinds of movies also trigger me. They piss me off, and the anger (and sometimes rage) is transformed into righteous action. I remember the first time I saw the original television miniseries Roots in 1977. I believe I was in about the third grade. I had heard my great-grandmother Rachel's stories of slavery from my grandmother. I remember one story in particular because she told it often. She'd say how the white folks treated her mama so bad. They talked to her like she was an animal. Beneath them. My grandmother was a devout Pentecostal Christian and so she'd say white folks were full of nothing but the devil. She talked about how tired and thirsty she'd be while walking alongside her mother in the cotton fields as they both picked cotton. My grandmother hated those times and she'd tell that story every chance she got.

I didn't have the mental capacity to even begin to understand the horrendous conditions my great-grandmother endured. I never got to meet her, so when my grandmother told us stories about her mother, it seemed like she was just a figment of my imagination. A superhero icon of some sort. Outside of this particular story, my grandmother and mother didn't often talk about my great-grandmother. I find it strange that I didn't see a photo of her until I was an adult. Nevertheless, I always pictured her as a superwoman. She had to be a strong and resilient woman to endure those times. Chattel slavery was one of the most sadistic and inhumane acts of white terrorism, and if my ancestors endured that, then I choose to find the resiliency to endure the challenges in my life.

Hearing about the enslavement of African people was depressing, but seeing it played out on television was maddening. My mind was blown when I watched Roots. It was horrific and painful to watch, but I kept tuning in for each episode. It pissed me the hell off. Don't trip! If you watched the miniseries as a kid, you know you went to school the next day mad as hell, looking at white folks like, "Don't even say one word, or else!" I must admit, I was angry at all white people. I think this was the first time in my life I felt pure and justified rage against them. Apparently, I was living in a protected bubble before viewing Roots. And now that I think about it, I don't recall my mother talking to me much about slavery when I was a child. I'm sure she was trying to protect my childhood innocence, but part of me wishes I had known more about my ancestral history earlier in my life. And I wish my grandmother and mother had told me more stories about how they survived being black back in the day.

I didn't crave those stories then, but now that I know my life's purpose, I understand how much the stories matter, and I long for them. They matter because when this brutal world and the beast of white terrorism tries to steal the breath from our beautiful black bodies, sometimes the only thing we can do is call on our creator, God, the divine one, and our ancestors who've been breathless before us. My God! How did black people survive chattel slavery? Sure, I realize it was either survive or die, but no words will ever adequately describe the relentless resiliency required for existence and survival. I know black women were sick and tired of being sick and tired, and yet for centuries of captivity they chose to rise from the ashes of terror with every desperate breath.

I'm convinced this radical and relentless resiliency has been passed down through our DNA and logged into our psyches and muscle memories. How could it not be? I believe it's transmitted to us through storytelling, matriarchal modeling, and epigenetics. What stories of resiliency did your mother, grandmothers, and aunties tell you? And without saying a word, how did the black women in your life embody this resiliency? Did you witness them being sick and tired of being sick and tired, yet in the same breath, going on about their business and getting shit done? Is this resiliency something to be celebrated or denounced? Is it a blessing or a curse? I believe it can be both.

When you're sick and tired of being sick and tired and don't stop to take care of yourself, it is certainly not a blessing. When you've worked yourself to the bone and don't stop to relax, it is detrimental to your health. When you keep ignoring the pain, and when you keep pressing through your exhaustion, you are participating in your own death. Slow, unintentional death, but death nonetheless, whether it be spiritual, emotional, and/or physical death. In all these cases, this kind of keep-going-no matter-what resiliency is a curse. I tend to refer to it as a generational curse. One that must be broken and not passed on to future generations of black women. My mom scuffled for decades, and I am so grateful that I can help her financially so she doesn't have to scuffle so hard anymore. Now she can finally relax and just enjoy her life.

What do you know about scuffling? Ha! If you don't know what that word means, let me illustrate it for you. Scuffling. I heard my mother say it all the time. And as I watched her do it, a big part of me vowed to never have to scuffle, although I've had my scuffling moments in past years. I've had to borrow money from my mother, had to take out high-interest cash loans to make ends meet, and had to move in with my mother as an adult when finances got tight. My scuffle didn't look like my mother's, but nevertheless, I scuffled! Scuffling is exhausting, and it can be embarrassing and humiliating too. Even though my mother spent much of her life scuffling, she always made space for other folks who were scuffling, who were just trying to survive. This is what black women do. We give even when our cups are empty.

From the time my mother's feet hit the floor in the morning until she laid her head on her pillow at night, she was making it happen. As she would say, she often made a way out of no way. When I say "make it happen," I mean cooking, cleaning, taking care of the kids, paying the bills, and managing a household on a measly fixed income. She received the same amount of money each month in the form of a disability check that did not cover all the household expenses. Running, caring for, and maintaining our home was her full-time job, and as I said in Chapter One, she took it seriously. Scratching and surviving! That's what she often called it. There wasn't a day that went by that my mother was not striving to win against the odds. And they were stacked high against her. According to society's white supremacist standards, she was destined to fail.

My mother was a trauma survivor. She was a dark-skinned, plus-sized woman. She was a single parent of two children with two different fathers. She was physically disabled due to a back injury in her early twenties. She was economically poor. She lived on a fixed income. She was financially dependent on state assistance. She was a recipient of housing assistance and food stamps. She received energy assistance for her utilities. She was a high school dropout. She is black. She is a woman. The system is not set up for a poor, "uneducated," disabled, black woman to win. Never. Ever. But my mama scratched and survived to live to tell about it today. She is the definition of resilient!

I remember my mother doing all kinds of things I thought were strange at the time. She would save her coins, and many times she sent us to the store with a pocketful of change to get what we needed. I hated having to spend all that change; it was embarrassing. I vowed to never have to save coins, only to find myself doing just that during a financially rough time in my life. But when I took those coins to the store as an adult, there was no shame in my game, because my mama had taught me how to scratch and survive to make a way out of no way. We don't always value the teaching of our elders and ancestors until we are presented with situations where we have nothing to call on but the black woman wisdom passed on to us by the resilient black women in our lives. Trust me, I too know how to scratch and survive when it's time to do so, and I am grateful for this wisdom. Shit! I wouldn't be here today, as the woman I am, without my mama's scratching and surviving.

I'm glad my mama is still here teaching me and sharing her wisdom generously, both directly and vicariously. Let white folks tell it, she should not have made it to see today, but she's still here. She's seventy-two as I write this book, and I'm happy to say she no longer scuffles financially. For the past four years I've prayed one simple prayer: "God use me. Bless me to be a blessing to the world and to bless my family." God is good, and my prayers have been answered. I am in a place where I can help my mother pay her bills and provide the things she not only needs but desires. It's an indescribable feeling to be able to not only support my family without struggle, but also to make sure the last days of my mother's life are scuffle-free! She deserves it, and I am grateful for her love, guidance, and wisdom. She's at an age where rising from the ashes is more challenging, so until she takes her last breath, I will be the wind beneath her wings.

* * * * * * * *

Racism and white supremacy created a heinous system perfectly designed to kill the black woman's spirit, black people's spirits. And every day, you defy the f*ck out of that system to not only rise from the ashes, but also to soar and thrive. You don't just rise automatically. The rise is the result of your courage and emotional resiliency. You are brave enough to get back up when you fall down or are pushed down. You have the internal flexibility to bounce back from your falls, and the emotional fortitude to keep on keeping on when it's the last thing you want to do. And not because your family, friends, and the world need you, but because you need you! I need you to get back up again and again, and to continue to rise higher into your black woman badassery. This you need to do for yourself! I need you to need you.

Why? Because your existence matters. You are valuable. You are worthy. You exist for a reason. You're here to do something meaningful. Born with a special assignment to complete. And your meaningful thing and special assignment do not have to be grand events. Your existence could be to resist, persist, and break the generational stronghold that has been gripping and suffocating your family legacy. Your existence could be to give love to those hungry for it. Your existence could be to open doors for others. It could be to shut down systems of oppression and change the world. I don't know why you exist, but I do know you are not a mistake. You are not an anomaly. There was no coincidence in your creation! You are here for a purpose, on purpose. I need you to digest and metabolize this truth, Sis!

Listen. Whether you're struggling right now or you're scuffling to survive the oppressive systems that try to strangle your significance, you need to know you deserve more. You deserve to thrive. You deserve to be safe and free. You deserve to be liberated and loved. You deserve to be happy and healed. You deserve to be protected and prosperous. You deserve whatever you desire. I know society in all its f*cked up ways may tell you otherwise, but I'm here to remind you that you are *Unf*ckablewith*, and f*ck what other people say you deserve and don't deserve! And while white society may have its foot on your back, you still get to choose what you deserve. And have it, too, if you damn well please!

Freedom and liberation will not be given to you. You have to seize it. And sometimes it requires you getting to the point of being sick and tired of being sick and tired, and then continuing on anyway, like Fannie Lou Hamer (Townsend) did. Fannie Lou was always tough and resilient. She began picking cotton at the age of six, and by the age of thirteen (and although she had a disfigured leg due to polio), she could pick between two hundred and three hundred pounds of cotton a day. But Fannie Lou was also rebellious by nature. She had a radical spirit that seemed to strengthen and support her resiliency and resolve. She grew up to become a voting rights, women's rights, and civil rights activist, and she finally snapped, so to speak. Fannie Lou's resiliency for scratching and surviving had been stretched to the max. But she refused to stay knocked down, and she was known for her civil rights activism until she took her last breath. And she was relentless in the fight for human rights for black people in Mississippi and nationally.

In 1962, Fannie Lou heard about the constitutional right to vote, and she immediately took action by joining the civil rights movement and traveling to Indianola, Mississippi with other black folks to try to register to vote. Of course white folks weren't having it, so they made it difficult for black folks, many of whom couldn't read or write, to register and cast their vote. When she returned from this trip to the plantation where she worked, the white overseer demanded that Fannie Lou withdraw her voter's registration. She refused, and she was fired and kicked off the plantation. While she was transient and displaced from her husband, Fannie Lou was threatened and shot at sixteen times by white supremacists.

One of the most horrendous things that happened to Fannie Lou Hamer occurred when she was arrested for attempting to eat in a café that didn't want to serve black people. She was taken to the county jail, and while there, a white male state trooper ordered two black inmates to beat her repeatedly with a black jack. When she screamed, they beat her harder. She was also sexually fondled during the incident. This brutality lasted for hours, and it left her with a blood clot over her eye, damaged kidneys, and horrific psychological wounds. It took over a month for Fannie Lou to recover from this vicious attack, and she didn't ever recover completely.

Fannie Lou suffered this inhumane and racist treatment because she wanted to vote. Because she wanted to be treated like a first-class citizen. Because she wanted to assert her right to be treated like a human being. I can't imagine the emotional and physical fortitude required to endure such savage treachery. I know Fannie Lou was sick and tired. Dog tired.

The assault didn't stop her, though. Fannie Lou dug deep inside and found the strength, courage, and resiliency to keep speaking truth to power. She kept on fighting for the rights of women and black people in the face of great hate and real danger. She didn't give up. She was relentless in her pursuit of liberty, justice, and freedom for black humanity. There's so much more I can share and honor about Fannie Lou Hamer. Yet what is most important to highlight is that you and I have rights and liberties today because of strong and resilient black women like Fannie Lou Hamer. Beat down. Exhausted. Emotionally devastated. Sick and tired. Fannie Lou rose from the ashes of white terrorism by holding on to a strand of resiliency to become the fire that tried to kill her. She refused to continue to be sick and tired, and instead remained grounded in these fundamental beliefs and truths: that she and other black folks deserved to be treated fair and just, and that they deserved to have their rights as full citizens. Fannie Lou Hamer refused to accept nothing less than what she deserved. Now that is black woman badassery! Are you accepting less than you deserve?

Resiliency shows up in another way that maybe you haven't considered. In my book *Unleash Your Significance*, I talk about your deserve level, what it is, and how to strengthen and raise it. Chapter Six of that book contains this passage:

> Your deserve level is a combination of the internal images you have of yourself, your self-esteem, what you believe to be true

about you and a culmination of the internal messages (beliefs) you have about yourself based on other people's opinions. This psycho-emotional concoction draws the deserve line in your mind, and until you intentionally do the mental work to raise the line, you'll feel unworthy of what you really deserve. You can start now. Change won't happen overnight, but with daily practice, you WILL raise your deserve level. And until you raise it, you will continue to settle, and it will be difficult for you to create your "more" and enjoy it.

—Catrice M. Jackson

Are you suffering from Deserve Atrophy? Your deserve level is just like a muscle. And as my Gran would say, "If you don't use it, you'll lose it." She meant that if you don't move your muscles, they atrophy and become weak. Deserve Atrophy is the weakening of your worthiness. People who believe they deserve the things they desire, and then get those things, have a strong deserve muscle. It may not always have been strong, but they have exercised that muscle to the point where they now expect to get what they deserve and are not afraid to flex it. In the description above, I mention a deserve line. What I mean by that is a "deserve threshold." For example, have you ever had someone praise you so much that it made you emotionally—and maybe even physically—uncomfortable? When they "over" praise you, do you wish they would stop, or do you try to minimize their praise with self-deprecating comments? Is there a tiny little voice inside that says, *I do not deserve all this praise?*

I admit this can be uncomfortable. I recently had a friend state several times during a phone conversation how much they appreciated my support of them and their family. They were deeply grateful and humble and kept saying, "You just don't know how much you mean to me." The humility expressed each time was palpable. The first time they said it, I received it easily because I love and appreciate grateful people. The next two or three times they said it, I could feel my body getting tense. That little "I don't deserve all this praise" voice was getting louder. But I consciously chose to relax into the discomfort of receiving praise to flex my deserve muscle. I did this for two reasons: first, because it was important for me to allow them the moment to express their gratitude, and second, because it strengthened my deserve level. Did I deserve this praise? Yes, so I shouldn't run from it. And I can accept it and be humble. I am worthy of praise, and so are you. I share this story as one example of how important it is for you to BELIEVE that you deserve whatever you desire.

Now let me say this: I'm highly aware that systems of oppression and the anti-blackness you experience are real challenges and can create barriers to you having what you really desire. I know racism and discrimination often dictate how society determines what you deserve and don't deserve. Until white supremacy is demolished and abolished, those challenges and barriers will always exist. Do you realize how resilient you are to survive this type of oppression every day? The fact that you exist is proof of your resiliency in the face of daily attacks on your mind, body, and spirit. And because you are equipped with the uncanny, innate ability to persist, you can strengthen your deserve muscle to experience what you desire and deserve. The same system that was set up to destroy my mother still exists to destroy you, but only if you let it. You must resist allowing oppression to suppress your desires. You must resist every prediction and affliction the world casts upon you. You can rise from the ashes when you raise your deserve level!

On a scale from one to ten, let's examine your current deserve level, with one being "I don't deserve anything" and ten being "I deserve everything I desire." Is the number you've given yourself high, low, or neutral? Now give a number to your self-esteem. Is the number closer to one ("I suck") or ten ("I am phenomenal")? How about how much you care what other people think of you? Rate that too. Is the number closer to one ("I worry a lot about what other people think") or ten ("I will unapologetically be me")? Look at those numbers. What do they say to you? How do you interpret them? Do you have some work to do to believe you deserve more, to feel better about yourself, and to not be concerned with what other people think about you? It will take conscious, intentional daily inner work, but you can do it.

You can move your threshold of worthiness higher by strengthening and flexing your deserve muscle. And if you settle for where you are, who you are, and what you experience, you are inevitably and willingly agreeing to Deserve Atrophy. You are saying yes to mediocrity and misery instead of manifesting your magic! Don't settle, Sis, unless you are completely and undeniably satisfied with who you are and the life you are experiencing right now. And if you are, I congratulate and celebrate you! If not, there's more for you. And you get to decide what your "more" will look like, and better yet, what it will feel like. So let's talk a little bit about worthiness. I prefer the word "worthy" to "self-love." Some folks would say self-love is vain, and others would say it is essential for living a joyful and satisfying life.

Some synonyms for the word "love" include adore, admire, appreciate, cherish, and respect. And when you believe you are worthy, you adore yourself, admire who you are, appreciate your imperfections, cherish your existence, and respect yourself. This is not vanity. This is honoring and valuing the masterpiece of a creation that you are. This is self-preservation. Worthiness is more than a survival strategy, it is a life source, a lifeline. Test this truth out. Think about the people you know who lack self-love or don't feel worthy of love, respect, or adoration.

How do they show up?

What kind of life are they living, truly?

How do other people treat them?

How does the world treat them?

I don't know a single person fitting this description that is genuinely happy or deeply satisfied. I conclude that they may be suffering from Deserve Atrophy. Somewhere deep down inside, they don't believe they deserve to be happy and deeply satisfied.

For generations, black women have mastered the art of being strong and resilient. You've learned how to do this to survive and sometimes thrive. When are you going to master the art of worthiness? The art of putting yourself first? The art of self-love? The art of adoration, admiration, and appreciation, by any means necessary? Do you value yourself this way? Do you have this kind of resiliency? The kind that no matter what other people say, you keep rising? The kind that no matter how many bricks are thrown at you, they just bounce off, and you keep rising?

It's okay to be sick and tired of being sick and tired, and there's no shame in scuffling. It's even better to flex your deserve muscles so you can thrive. You may not be where you want to be in life. You may not be experiencing everything you desire. But this I know for sure: you can be extraordinary right now, at your current level, until you get to your next level.

You can be Unf*ckablewith now.

Use your resiliency to rise.

Use your resiliency to serve your highest good.

You deserve whatever the hell you want.
Start flexing those deserve muscles!
Don't forget, Sis, you are magic in motion.
Rise!

Writing Prompts to Rise from the Ashes

How do you define resiliency?

_____

_____

_____

_____

_____

_____

_____

_____

Has your resiliency been more of a blessing or a curse?

_____

_____

_____

_____

_____

_____

_____

_____

What do you believe you deserve?

_____

_____

_____

_____

_____

_____

_____

How have you had to scuffle, scratch, and survive? What did it teach you?

_____

_____

_____

_____

_____

_____

What do you deeply desire and crave?

_____

_____

_____

_____

_____

_____

_____

What gold have you mined from your ancestors' resiliency?

_____

_____

_____

_____

_____

_____

_____

_____

_____

How will you use your resiliency to rise?

_____

_____

_____

_____

_____

_____

_____

_____

_____

MADAM CJ WALKER

INGENIOUS

"I got my start by giving myself a start."

Madame C.J. Walker

* * * * * * * *

CHAPTER FOUR

INGENIOUS

I come from a line of women who could rub two dimes together to make a dollar. Women who made something out of nothing and did it fabulously and relentlessly! Women who knew how to stretch meals, delay bills, and hold it down by any means necessary. Women who were weary, yet always found a way to win and give love. Women who got it done with or without a man. Women who scuffled, shuffled, and shifted so I could exist to become their wildest dreams. Women who used what God gave them so they could give blessings to their families they never received themselves. Praying women. Faithful women. Loving women. Strong women. Brilliant women. Ingenious women. Badass black women!

Playing at my grandmother's house when I was a kid—especially if I also got to spend the night—was one of the highlights of my life. My Gran seemed to have a remedy for every challenge and knew how to make things just right. When I had a stomach ache, she gave me a peppermint candy. You know them old peppermints she'd have at the bottom of her purse! When I was constipated, she served me up a nasty teaspoon of cod liver oil. When she ran out of toothpaste, she dipped my toothbrush into a box of baking soda. And let's not forget about the infamous hot toddies she'd make when I was sick. (I didn't realize back then that she was often adding a shot of liquor to those hot drinks. They knocked me right out after a few sips!) When I was congested, she'd fill a small cooking pot with water, add a teaspoon of Vick's VapoRub, set it on the heat vent, and before I knew it, I could breathe easily again.

It seemed like no matter what problem I had, my Gran had the best solutions! As a young girl, I often looked up at her in complete awe of her brilliance. She was so wise, and so generous with her wisdom. She was always teaching me something, either deliberately or vicariously. My Gran couldn't read very well, but one thing is for sure: she knew her biblical scriptures. And yes, no matter what I was going through, she had the perfect scripture to either put things into clearer perspective or empower me to keep hope alive. Sometimes, like Tyler Perry's Madea character, she'd mix and match scriptures to get her point across. Hell, I didn't know any better. It made perfect sense to me back then. My Gran was a God-loving, hallelujah-shouting, several-times-a-week-church-going fieryand feisty woman. She loved her some church!

My Gran was a heavy-set woman, so she often had difficulty fastening her brassiere and zipping her dresses. When I wasn't around to help her put on her clothes, she would attach a safety pin and a piece of string onto her zipper so she could zip herself up. Speaking of zippers, when one of them got stuck, she'd wipe a little Vaseline or Crisco on it and it was as good as new. Boom! I thought my Gran was magic! She was. I used to laugh at her trying to squeeze into her girdles and she would laugh right along with me. It took forever to get her all packed in because we deep belly laughed the whole time. She loved to laugh. I sure do miss her laughter. I miss my Gran.

I used to love helping my Gran get dressed for church. I would browse around and delight in looking through her jewelry boxes while sneaking a spray or two of perfume. Her dresser was overflowing with all kinds of beautiful perfume bottles, oils, and scented creams. It seemed like every time I was in her bedroom there was more to explore. She had antique-looking jewelry boxes filled with pierced and clip-on earrings, colorful necklaces, pins, and shiny brooches. She had so many varieties of accessories, including scarves, pocketbooks (as she called them), and her favorite church-going hats. My Gran loved to adorn her crown with wraps, turbans, and the most glorious hats I had ever seen. Man... could she rock a hat! When she'd finish getting all gussied up for church, sometimes I would just look at her in complete amazement. My Gran didn't have a lot of money, but she looked like a movie star!

She encouraged my curiosity unless I got in her special drawers. I don't even know what was in those drawers, but when my Gran said don't mess with stuff, I left stuff alone. When I reflect on the moments spent with my Gran, we were either being silly in her bedroom or I was watching her cook and enjoying meals with her in the kitchen. My Gran could burn, as the old folks say. She loved to cook, and I learned to cook just by watching her work her magic without recipes. One of my favorite things she made was banana pudding. She made it from scratch. It was so thick, rich, and decadent. I've yet to taste anything like my Gran's banana pudding. To this day I reminisce about it and wish I had her recipe. We sat together in the old-fashioned restaurant booth in her kitchen countless times, sharing love through food. She loved to eat too!

There was something splendid and adventurous about spending time with my Gran. She had her own kind of genius. Today I fully recognize and honor her ingenious spirit. I see the same creative spirit in my mother, and I know it lives within me too. There aren't many things that my mother can't create. When it came to interior design, she was unmatched. Even at seventy-two, she is still infatuated with beautifying her home. And although I've relaxed my obsession with "keeping house," how my home is adorned and decorated matters to me. A lot. Sometimes I'm amazed at my own creativity. The first time I tried painting, I surprised myself by creating a picture of a black woman with big, bright, hypnotic eyes, voluptuous red lips, and an Afro that cascaded off the canvas. She was glorious! I'm so thankful that my mother's and grandmother's ingenuity and creativity was passed on to me.

I often wish I could travel back in time to bear witness to the journey and experiences of my matriarchal ancestors. I wish I could have met my great-grandmother Rachel and my great-great-grandmother Harriet. From what my grandmother told me, Rachel was a fiery black woman too. As I mentioned in the previous chapter, my grandmother would often share memories of walking alongside my great-grandmother in the fields as they picked cotton. I can't even begin to imagine what that must have been like. Yet I'm deeply grateful for the ingenious spirit, the will to survive, and the know-how the women in my family possessed, otherwise I might not be here today. Their black woman resiliency is part of the reason why I rise again and again.

* * * * * * *

Damn! How did our matriarchs survive their terrible times? What I do know, Black Women, is that we are a brilliant and ingenious tribe of women. I won't get all biblical on you, but I believe with every fiber of my being that black people are the chosen people. I believe all life has come through the original black woman's womb. I believe black women are the epitome of strength, courage, and wisdom. I believe this not only because we had to survive unfathomable treachery, but also because we had the ingenuity and resilience to do so. Black women have survived every possible human tragedy. And still we rise out of the ashes, emerging like black phoenixes, harnessing every defeat and spiritual attack to ascend as stronger and more powerful people. Ain't nothing like black women rising!

I believe we are supernatural and that ingenuity is part of our magic. Black Women, we ARE ingenious magic in motion. This is true no matter what kind of black woman you are. It doesn't matter if you're a formally educated black woman or a street-smart savvy black woman. It doesn't matter if you are light-, dark-, or brown-skinned. It doesn't matter if you've got wavy locs or tight curls. It doesn't matter if you grew up in the hood or the suburbs. Married, single, or divorced—it doesn't matter. There's something magical in the melanin of black women:

A pray-and-don't-faint kind of magic

An anchor-in-the-middle-of-the-storm kind of magic

A make-a-way-out-of-no-way kind of magic

An endurance-and-longevity kind of magic

A beautiful struggle kind of magic

A bend-but-don't-break kind of magic

Damn! This black woman magic is both bitter AND sweet. What I love most about black woman magic is its diversity. I think we toss around the phrase "Black Girl Magic" as a generalized nod to black women without comprehending the vast distinctive divinity in their souls. Much like diamonds, each black woman's magic is unique and unparalleled. Do you know what makes your magic unique and unparalleled? Do you know what makes your magic distinctive and like no other black woman's? And do you know how divine your magic is?

Although I believe we are magical, we're also delicate and beloved beings who need to be cared for and who need to care for one another. One of the themes that rings true as I reflect on the lives of the black women I know and love is that they often put their needs, wants, and desires last. Over the years I've witnessed my mother use her ingenuity, but not for herself. Instead she used it to take care of other people's kids, allow dislocated people to stay in her home, and worry herself almost to death over other people's shit. She and I have talked numerous times about her detrimental caretaking. And every time we engage in this conversation, I tell her to stop taking on other people's problems and LIVE her life. Unfortunately, this bittersweet part of my mother's magic will be a part of who she is until she takes her last breath.

In a lot of ways, my mother and grandmother remind me of Sarah Breedlove, who later became known as Madame C.J. Walker. They weren't millionaires, but I'd say my grandmother created healing concoctions similar to Madame C.J. Walker's, and my mother was indeed an ingenious business woman. Sarah Breedlove was born on a Louisiana plantation in 1867 to enslaved parents Owen and Minerva Anderson Breedlove. At the age of seven, she was orphaned and worked as a farm laborer in the cotton fields of a nearby plantation in Vicksburg, Mississippi. At the age of fourteen, she married Moses McWilliams to escape the brutality of her brother-in-law, Jesse Powell. After her husband died, Sarah moved to St. Louis, Missouri and began working in a barber shop with her four brothers, where she earned about a dollar fifty per day.

Although she earned less than two dollars a day, Sarah was able to put her only daughter, A'Lelia Walker, through public school. When Sarah began to suffer from an unknown skin aliment on her scalp that caused her to lose most of her hair, she and her brothers experimented with various remedies to treat her hair loss. After trial and error, Sarah created Madame C.J. Walker's Wonderful Hair Grower, a scalp conditioner that also healed her ailment. According to Sarah, the idea to create this wonder cream came to her in a dream. Sarah Breedlove became Madame C.J. Walker after marrying her third husband, Charles Joseph Walker. She created her own business and began traveling throughout the South and Southeast, selling her amazing product door to door and doing product demonstrations.

By 1910, Walker had settled in Indianapolis, Indiana. There she built a factory where she mass-produced her wonder products, a manicure salon, and a school to train what she called "hair culturists." She expanded her business into the Caribbean and Central America and finally settled in New York, where she not only continued to oversee the operations of her business, but also became an activist in the black social and political scenes. Walker got heavily involved with the anti-lynching movement and the National Association for the Advancement of Colored People (NAACP), and she donated large sums of money to various causes.

In 1917, Madame C.J. Walker organized one of the first (if not the first) major conventions for businesswomen in Philadelphia called the Madame C.J. Walker's Hair Culturists Union of America. At this convention, Walker recognized the achievements and successes of her fellow culturists and encouraged them to take part in social and political movements. Hmm... kind of sounds like the Mary Kay empire, doesn't it (Ole Thieving Ass Becky)? Anyway, this was revolutionary at a time when black folks hadn't been free from the bondage of slavery very long, and many were scratching to survive. Before Madame C.J. Walker passed away, she created revolutionary hair care products for black people by using her passion, tenacity, and ingenuity. Walker was a badass black woman trailblazer who turned her problem into profit and used her ingenuity to ignite a movement for future black women business owners. Thank God for Madame C.J. Walker. What a way to turn homemade remedies into revolutionary revenue while empowering other black women to rise! Walker is the epitome of rubbing two pennies together to make a dollar.

Like Madame C.J. Walker, my mother gave herself a start by giving herself a start. She refused to accept the limitations of her physical disability. She chose to shatter the lies that she was a throwaway who would never succeed because of her circumstances. She used every single gift God gave her to make a way out of no way. And over the years, I have watched her monetize her magic. My mom has created one-of-a-kind pieces of clothing, hosted fashion shows, and sold her creations before the models could undress. She's created art pieces and sold them for top dollar. She has done interior decorating and got paid well to do it. She's created gorgeous crafts and sold them to make ends meet. I don't remember a time in my life, until recently because of her age, when my mother wasn't using her ingenuity to solve her problems and create a way to survive and thrive. And even though she is not creating for profit today, she is still creating, because it's her magic and it brings her joy!

Like my mother and grandmother, I've mastered the scuffling, scratching, and surviving aspects of black womanhood because they were generational expectations and pseudo badges of honor. Badges I've chosen to retire. Generational curses I am breaking so my son does not have to scuffle and scratch to survive. If we want the next generations to be better and live better, we must be better and live better according to our own definitions. We must begin to break down the barriers in our lives. We must shatter the remaining shackles on our feet.

We must abolish those curses and use our ingenuity to create new rules, expectations, and guiding principles for our seeds and future generations. Otherwise, we will continue to pass down the poison that paralyzes the black community and pits us against each other. Now don't get me wrong. Character building occurs in the scratching and scuffling, but so does character breaking. When folks stay in a perpetual state of struggle, it stifles their growth, and a spirit of settling sets in. I believe it is difficult to be *Unf*ckablewith* if you settle.

I choose to use my curiosity and creativity to actualize my magic. Will you? I choose to build my character instead of breaking it. Will you? I choose to pour out the poison. Will you? I choose to not settle. Will you? I choose to be *Unf*ckablewith*. Will you? You can see the honor in the struggle without demonizing it, and you can choose to dream and actualize a bigger and better vision for yourself. You can want more, and you can expect it and demand it. Despite the bricks the world throws at you, and no matter what barriers may be standing in your way, one thing I believe is that ingenuity can take you a step farther and carry you through. I have found great value and success in using creativity to get over the bumps in my life and to break through barriers.

When I have been in a financial slump and needed money, I have often created something to monetize. My go-to question was always, "How can I get creative to solve this problem?" Followed by, "What do I need and who can help me?" This was my version of rubbing two dimes together to make a dollar. This was me using my ingenuity to make a way out of no way. To make something happen. To survive, and sometimes to thrive. What can you create, Sis? How can you reach down into your divine magic and make a way out of no way? What glorious gifts have you not tapped into yet? Your creator made you; you are not ill-equipped. You have what you need. Get busy. Find and use your magic and gifts to take the next step and get to the next level. Do you know who you come from? You come from imaginative, innovative, and inventive black women. It's in your DNA. Tap into the resources that lie within you.

When I became curious and creative, most times I could solve any problem I was facing. And other times I just had to wade in the weary water and dredge through it, struggling to make it to dry land. There were times I went under, but when I had the strength and determination to rise up, I got creative, and that took me another step forward. My Gran always said, "Girl, don't give up. Give out." I realize now she meant there was a fire inside of me even when I felt like I was drowning. She meant there was another breath and another step inside of me even when I wanted to quit. She meant there was hope and determination inside of me, and I needed to dig deep into my reservoir of magic and bring it to the surface. To make it over. To make it through. When I look back on the horrible moments in my life, especially when I didn't think I could survive them, somehow I found a way to give out and not give up. No matter what you're facing right now, don't give up, give out!

Listen. We are HERE because our mamas, aunties, and grannies were wise, resourceful, and ingenious. We have learned and inherited their ingenuity. And we stand on the shoulders of mighty and magical black women who continuously rose from their ashes into their black woman badassery! Your magic is inherent. You don't have to be ingenious like me or the women I talk about in this book, but you can choose to unleash your unique genius to create the life you want. To be *Unf*ckablewith*, you must repeatedly exercise the power of yes and the potency of no.

There is freedom in saying no.

There is honor in saying yes to yourself.

There is liberation in not letting other folks' emergencies become your priority.

There is deliverance in putting your self-care at the top of your list.

There is LIFE in setting boundaries, holding strong to your expectations, and teaching people how to treat you.

Black women, we are ingenious.

I swear, black women are the most brilliant and creative people I know.

And Sis, you are one of those creative and magical black women.

Rise up from your ashes!

Writing Prompts to Rise from the Ashes

What does ingenuity look like for you?

_____

_____

_____

_____

_____

_____

_____

_____

How do you use creativity to survive and thrive?

_____

_____

_____

_____

_____

_____

_____

_____

What did your grandmothers teach you?

_____

_____

_____

_____

_____

_____

_____

How can you tap into the ingenuity of your ancestors to create the life you desire?

_____

_____

_____

_____

_____

_____

_____

How will you better honor your gift of ingenuity?

_____

_____

_____

_____

_____

_____

What boundaries do you need to put in place so you can create?

_____

_____

_____

_____

_____

_____

_____

_____

_____

_____

How can you use ingenuity to rise from your ashes?

_____

_____

_____

_____

_____

_____

_____

_____

_____

_____

"You can't be hesitant about who you are."

Viola Davis

* * * * * * * *

CHAPTER FIVE

MAGICAL

I used to be willfully ignorant in my younger years. I was sick and extremely infected with the lethal virus of white terrorism. Most of us learn at a young age that the closer your skin color is to whiteness, the "better" you are, and I was no exception. This deceptive delusion ain't nothing new. White folks have been indoctrinating black folks with this treacherous fairy tale since forever. I used to believe my proximity to whiteness was something to brag about and be proud of. Now I know just how poisonous that proximity is. When I was in high school, I believed I was better than my darker sisters, although there were a few I deemed "pretty for dark-skinned girls." Even when my anti-black antics weren't explicit and overt, light-skinned superiority always lurked under the surface of my seemingly accepting smile.

I judged other black girls by the tone of their skin, the texture of their hair, and the shapes of their facial features. Dark skin, nappy hair, and big lips were unattractive to me. I wasn't outright mean to black girls who looked like that, I just didn't give them much time or invite them into my inner circle. I disregarded and dismissed their presence. I intentionally chose to not befriend them. My covert anti-blackness was just as violent as overt racism, but I felt justified in my beliefs because according to both black and white society, they were valid.

The media justified my beliefs because they rarely portrayed dark-skinned people on television. And when they did, those folks were villainized and criminalized. Magazines justified my beliefs because it was rare to see dark-skinned women grace their covers. Conversations I had with other light-skinned girls justified my beliefs because they shared my f*cked up beliefs. Hell, my own mother made negative comments about dark-skinned people occasionally, and she was dark-skinned herself. And when your mama says it, it has to be true, right?

Wrong! Hell to the no! Absolutely, unequivocally wrong! I know this today, but back when I was young, impressionable, and ignorant, I fed into and believed these horrible anti-black stereotypes, and regretfully, I harmed my sisters. This is just one example of how even black women harm black women. We are not safe from anyone, and we can be our own worst nightmares. It probably took me over a decade before I could see and label my own anti-blackness. Even in my early thirties, I still caught myself perpetuating anti-black stereotypes, especially related to how other black women spoke, dressed, and acted in public. I would turn my nose up in disgust and embarrassment when black women were what I deemed too loud, ghetto, angry, indignant, and/or inarticulate.

Why? All for the white gaze. To remain closer to the proximity of whiteness. Because I was misinformed and uneducated. Because I knew white folks were watching the behavior of these black women and sizing me up to see whether I was like them. And I didn't want to be. Because I was well-educated, articulate, and took pride in being a black woman who defied the stereotypes. Because I refused to scuffle and scratch to survive. Because I thought I was a magical negro. Because I thought if I acted differently, I would be treated differently, and sometimes I was. Because I was suffering from proximity poison and didn't know it.

In a lot of ways, I was asleep. I had been fed the lies of toxic whiteness, gobbled them up, and digested and metabolized them to the detriment of myself and others. And I had the damn nerve to regurgitate that verbal vomit to my son in his early years. Disgusting! I am not that person any longer. I am becoming educated and am searching for the truth. My consciousness is shifting, and I work daily to liberate myself from the lies that have been forced down my throat. I now know better, and therefore, I am better and do better. I'm waking up! And I am re-educating my son and educating my grandson about toxic whiteness. I'm teaching them how to reject their own anti-blackness so they too can be liberated and free.

My wakeup call happened in 2008. I was the racial justice director for a non-profit organization and was in charge of the anti-racism training offered to the community. I excelled in the position and felt like I was operating in my inherent gifts. I loved my job until I had to provide white privilege training for the staff. Before that, they loved me and my work. I received a lot of applause and accolades for educating "those white folks out there." But their love quickly dissolved and transformed into violent fragility when I created a class for them to confront their own white privilege and anti-blackness. After the entire staff went through the training, all hell broke loose. Many of my co-workers stopped talking to me and asking me out to lunch, and they avoided me at all costs. I was being punished and penalized for doing my job—and for doing it exceptionally well, I might add.

The culture of this predominantly white women environment became lethal. Literally. The stress of doing the work and dealing with white woman violence, microaggressions, discrimination, and white fragility started to affect my health. I experienced irritable bowel syndrome (IBS) and frequent cold sore flare-ups. I began dreading going to work and felt angry, isolated, and ostracized. Years prior to this time, I had discovered I am anemic, and had been prescribed low-dose iron pills. I was advised to take them for the rest of my life. On a Friday in December 2007, I went in for a routine checkup with my primary care physician. I had not been taking my iron pills consistently, and I knew she was going to get on my case about it. I expected my iron levels to be low and planned on stopping by the drugstore after my appointment to refill my prescription.

After I arrived home, my doctor called me and told me to get back to her office right away. When I got there, she informed me that my hemoglobin level was dangerously low. The normal range for women is 12.0 to 15.5, but mine was 7. Hemoglobin is a protein that is responsible for transporting iron-containing oxygen in the red blood cells to your lungs and other major organs. Because my level was low, my major organs were not getting enough oxygen. They were compromised, and thus were working harder than necessary, causing stress and exhaustion. I'll never forget that moment: my doctor told me I was literally walking dead. She couldn't believe I had not collapsed or passed out.

My doctor was adamant that I should not try to increase my levels by taking iron pills; doing so would take too long. My vital organs were at risk. My life was in danger. She suggested I get a blood transfusion. At first, I refused. I refused because my mother and grandmother had taught me it was a sin in the eyes of God for humans to take bodily fluids and organs from one another. I wanted to live, and I wanted to obey God. I wanted to adhere to what I had been taught and believed. I had a spiritual decision to make. Do I risk my life and obey God, or do I save my life and ask for forgiveness? I chose to have the blood transfusion. I wanted to live. I needed to live. My son, my only child, was a sophomore in high school at the time, and there was no way in hell I was going to die before he was grown.

The stress of the job, the violent white fragility, the IBS, and the low iron were trying to take me out. I thought about the times my grandmother had said to not give up, but to give out. After talking it over with my husband, looking into the face of my beloved son, and spending time in deep prayer, I chose to receive someone else's blood. I chose to live. I had to stay overnight in the hospital. And as I struggled through this moral and spiritual dilemma, I came to terms with my mortality. I made a vow to God that I would take this blood that gave me new life and live out my purpose. I made a vow to not let whiteness and white violence kill me. I made a vow to never give away my magic to white folks, who often want to use black people only for pleasure or profit. I made a vow to live out loud. I made a vow to be free of the white gaze. I made a vow to fulfill my destiny.

After deep reflection that weekend, I decided to resign from my job. I walked into the office that Monday with a sixty-day written notice of resignation and gave it to my supervisor. She was shocked. I didn't care. I was unwavering and unapologetic about my decision. Those last two months of employment were torturous. Once my colleagues found out I had resigned, they cared even less that I existed, and I cared even less about being there. February 8, 2008 was my last day of work. I walked out with my boxes of belongings and never looked back. It was scary. I didn't have a plan. I didn't have a significant amount of money saved, and I had no idea what my next steps would be. All I knew was that it was time to fulfill my lifelong dream of being an entrepreneur. I knew this for sure. I knew I would live free and liberated or die trying.

This was my wake-up call. In that moment, I had seen the smoke and mirrors for the lies and illusions they are. It doesn't matter how light-skinned you are. It doesn't matter how many degrees you have. It doesn't matter if you dress the part, walk the walk, and talk the white folks' talk. I was still black and my proximity to whiteness did not protect me. I am well-spoken, but that didn't stop the violence. I'm black, and there's a price to pay to be black and a woman in this world. An oppressive and often painful price. My light skin did not keep me safer than the darker-skinned black women I knew. I saw the poison for what it really is. This monumental moment helped me finally face my anti-blackness, and it helped me shift my beliefs about blackness and toxic whiteness.

I've been on my own personal purge of the vicious poison ever since. And each year I become stronger, wiser, and less anti-black. I still have work to do. I still slip into that ugly lie. But I catch myself quicker and try to stay vigilant to avoid causing harm to black folks. Toxic whiteness is so virulent and relentless that I'll be working to rid myself of this infection until I take my last breath. Today when I see black women who are angry, I understand why. When I see them going off in a store, I know why. When I hear all the different variations of black vernacular spoken out loud, I smile. When I see black women out in public unbothered by the invasive white gaze, I scream *yesss!* inside. When I see black women owning their magic and navigating their lives the way they choose, I say to myself, Yes, Sis, be *Unf*ckablewith*! I see and honor the magic in every black woman I encounter.

That Black Girl Magic! That melanin, though... it's magic for *real*, Sis.

Chocolate cocoa dipped in molasses.
Sun-kissed cinnamon brown.
Glistening midnight black.
Caramelized deep brown sugar.
Sweet honey glazed by God.
And every magnificent shade of blackness in between is beautiful
black girl melanin magic!

* * * * * * *

Black girl magic is more than a cliché, it's genetically glorious! I recently discovered that melanin is found in almost every organ in our bodies. It's necessary for nerve and brain function, vision, and cell reproduction. Who knew, right? Melanin is a warrior and fights off the free radicals that cause skin damage. Yesss! That's why black skin doesn't crack. But wait, back to the warrior part. The fight and fearlessness of us is literally and divinely encoded into our beautiful, magical, melanated blackness. Free radicals are treacherous and deadly cells that relentlessly try to harm and kill us. Yet the melanin in our skin goes gangsta on those radical cells to fight back and protect us. Our melanin is a bad mama jama!

It's no coincidence that these deadly cells are called radical. The word "radical" means these cells are a destructive threat to our fundamental nature. Free radicals have one detrimental agenda: to break us down, steal our youthfulness and vitality, and eventually kill us. Does this scenario sound familiar? Does anyone come to mind? Can you identify some free radical people in your lives that are a threat to your fundamental nature? Can you think of any folks who are trying to destroy and kill you? Sis, I know you can. And I know this destruction has been haunting you for your whole life. Brother Malcolm X was right when he stated, "The most disrespected person in America is the black woman. The most unprotected person in America is the black woman. The most neglected person in America is the black woman."

When hasn't there been a time in your black life when you were disrespected, unprotected, and neglected? Hell, I can't think of one yet, and I'm almost a half-century old. In this hateful hierarchy of life, black women have been at the bottom, scratching and surviving while carrying the weight of the world on our tired-ass backs. We've been the mammies, the work mules, the breadwinners, the concubines, the wet nurses, the maids, the freedom fighters, the nannies, and the load carriers of everyone's burdens, including our own. Free radical folks have tried to kill us at every turn since time began. Yet we fight back, we rise, we survive, and some of us thrive. Free radical folks who have tried to destroy us include white folks, non-black folks, and other black folks. Everyone has come for black women, including, most sadly, other black women.

How in the hell do we keep getting up? How do we keep rising from the ashes and dusting ourselves off again? Century after century, black women get emotionally and spiritually destroyed on a daily basis, yet still we rise. Everyone takes us for granted. Everyone! We take each other for granted. In every way imaginable, we are told to sit down, shut up, and stay in our place. Directly and indirectly, the world tells us we do not matter and to stop saying we do. They tell us to go to the back. They tell us to get out of the way. They tell us to wait our turn. They tell us to be seen and not heard. Some folks don't even want to experience our presence. And let's keep it real: often we do all this to each other, and still we rise. How? Why? What is it about black women that allows us to endure this destruction day in and day out and still rise? Because we are *Unf*ckablewith*, that's why!

Why are we *Unf*ckablewith*? It's got to be that melanin magic, that black girl magic. It's the only thing that makes sense to me. Fundamentally, we are genetically the same as every other woman who walks this planet. Yet there's something special about black women. And when I say, "black women," I'm talking about women with shades of black and brown skin with roots anchored in the motherland of Africa. It doesn't matter if you're Afro-Latina, Afro-Asian, or Afro-whatever. The magic is in that Afro part. I'm not dismissing the other parts of who you are, but hey, magically speaking, women with that Afro in them just have a different kind of magic. Magic that consists of strength, bravery, creativity, resourcefulness, and resiliency. Black women have been resisting and persisting since day one, no matter which continent we live on. Those destructive free radicals relentlessly keep coming for us, but we are not to be f*cked with!

Black women are magical. Gloriously magical. As I said in the previous chapter when I was talking about our ingenious magic, I think we've always known we are magic deep down inside. Now it's time to not only own it, but also to empower other black women to own and activate their magic. So, what does it mean to be magical? Of course the answer will be different for every black woman. Words like "breathtaking," "magnificent," "enchanting," "otherworldly," and "supernatural" come to mind when I think about the minds and souls of black women. I would be remiss if I didn't mention CaShawn Thompson. In 2013, this splendid black woman coined the phrase "Black Girl Magic" (originally #BlackGirlsAreMagic) and created the hashtag that sparked a movement of naming, honoring, and celebrating black women's ability to persevere despite adversity.

When I try to wrap my brain around the infinite resourcefulness and creativity within black women, it's mindboggling. I feel like I could spend the rest of my life defining what this magic means, and I still wouldn't be finished. Black women get shit done. Black women hold it down even when no one's holding them. And even though we get tired of enduring no matter what, the fact that we can is magical. Thank you, CaShawn. Black women may disagree about what it means to be magical, and some may believe this "magic" reinforces the work mule stereotype (and in some ways it does), but it is undeniable that we are magical!

History shows us that black women should not have survived what we have endured. But we have not only survived, we are some of the most brilliant and successful women in the world. Anything horrific that you can imagine happening to a woman since the beginning of time has happened to a black woman. Through centuries of chattel enslavement and decades of dehumanizing discrimination, black women have refused to stay down when knocked down. Many folks, including black women, don't know how we keep getting back up again. That's magic, Sis. Defying the obstacles and odds. Doing what folks said could never be done. Surviving and thriving through lifetimes of treachery. Experiencing joy when the world tries to strip you of your happiness in every breath. Turning dust into dreams. Loving when you never learned how to love. Listen... that's magic, Sis!

I cannot end this chapter without celebrating the black girl magic of the one and only badass Viola Davis. I love everything about her. She is truly shining in all her glory, but that is not how her story began. She was born in 1965 on her grandmother's farm on the Singleton Plantation in St. Matthews, South Carolina. She grew up in poverty, living in what she calls "rat-infested apartments" and experiencing quite a bit of family dysfunction, but she was still able to rise from her ashes. Why? How was she able to do this? And not just become a famous actress, but kill the game like no other in the way she uses her roles to personify her genius. Tenacity? Resiliency? What is it? I could probably write a whole chapter on Viola's magic. She completely mesmerizes me every time I see her in character.

But what I am most infatuated by is her authenticity. I love her down-to-earthness. Her raw passion for people and social justice issues. I love how she demands that the white gaze sees all her unfiltered blackness in her role as Annalise Keating on the TV show *How to Get Away with Murder*. From what I understand, she requests certain depictions of her blackness be shown without being whitewashed or glamorized. She is saying to the white gazers, "You gone see all this uncut, unpolished, unapologetic blackness when you look at my nappy hair and full black lips." And I love everything about her declaration that her blackness be seen and celebrated in all its gloriousness. Yes! Man, listen when I see her do her thing, I see black girl magic personified. And I'm here for it all the time. She's badass. She's figured out how to rise from her ashes into her Black Woman Badassery!

You may be thinking that Viola has some kind of advantage that you do not. And maybe she does; if so, I don't know about it. For me, she is just one of many examples of black women who endured horrible circumstances, yet somehow, in the deepest place in her soul, she knew she was beyond those circumstance. She believed she deserved better than what her eyes could see before her. She made up her mind that in spite of her circumstances, she was not going to wallow in the cesspool of poverty as she experienced it. I believe she knew her scratching and surviving would one day pay off. But what I believe most about Viola is that she knew what her magic was. She protected it. She adored it. She nurtured and cultivated it. Because I think she knew that in a world intentionally created to destroy her, it was all she had, and she had better protect it like it was worth a million dollars. It was. It is.

Listen. I know your circumstances are different than hers, mine, and every other black woman who will read this book. But the truth is the truth is the truth for every black woman, including me. WE ARE MAGIC. I AM MAGIC. YOU ARE MAGIC. The gifts, skills, and talents within you make you one of a freaking kind! Do you hear me? Do you feel me? You are pure genius. I need you to believe it like it's the only belief possible.

It's your magic that will help you defy the odds.

It's your magic that will help you heal.

It's your magic that will help you become the fire to take back your life from whatever and whomever is trying to steal it.

Sis, I need you to be like Viola. I need you to pinpoint your magic and then protect it, adore it, nurture it, and cultivate it because just like hers, your magic is priceless. Don't let the fire consume you, activate your magic and become the fire! And do not become hesitant about who you are.

There's something about black women that allows us to do the unimaginable, the unthinkable, and the impossible. That's magic. That's melanin magic. It's *Unf*ckablewith* black girl magic! Black girl magic is not a cliché. It's real. It's tangible and powerful. So what is magic? In my book *Unleash Your Significance*, I give explicit examples of the ways in which magic can be expressed and actualized. I share them again here:

* Magic is turning your words into experiences.

* Magic is moving a dream from distant thought to an intimate reality.

* Magic is making the invisible tangible and touchable.

* Magic is predicting how your life turns out.

* Magic is transforming your physical body and restoring your vitality.

* Magic is purging your soul from everything that paralyzes your purpose.

* Magic is doing work you love and loving the work you do.

* Magic is leaping out of your comfort zone into the unknown and thriving.

* Magic is turning limiting beliefs into limitless possibilities.

* Magic is creating harmony within and living your own unique melody.

* Magic is creating and experiencing moments that take your breath away.

* Magic is trusting your soul knows the way and following it.

* Magic is saying "so what" and living your life unapologetically.

* Magic is slowing down and savoring the silence and synchronicity of life.

* Magic is hearing the whispers of the divine one and saying "yes!"

* Magic is unleashing your gifts and serving the world with them.

* Magic is not giving a damn what other people think of you.

* Magic is making a meaningful contribution to humanity.

* Magic is fiercely loving you better than anyone else could ever love you.

* Magic is following your bliss and wallowing in all the goodness and splendor you can imagine.

* Magic is having peace of mind, love in your heart, and a generous spirit.

* Magic is deeply forgiving yourself and choosing to love and be loved again.

* Magic is being comfortable in your own skin and appreciating every magnificent part of you.

* Magic is thinking positive thoughts and showing up in the world with optimism.

* Magic is curiosity, creativity and answering the calling for your life.

Magic is unlimited! There are so many ways to create magic in your life in your own unique way. Please stop trying to duplicate other peoples' lives. You'll never live their dreams. You'll never walk their paths. You'll never carry out their purposes, and you'll never arrive at their destinations. Embrace the awesomeness of your originality, manifest your own dreams, confidently walk your own path, and live out your special destiny that's designed just for you! It's time to create some magic; are you ready? I love to look at creating magic this way: misery is existing, mediocrity is surviving, but MAGIC is living and thriving!

You have what I call multi-dimensional magic within you! There is a perfectly imperfect beautiful mosaic of magic inside you that only you possess. No one in the whole world has the magic recipe you hold in your soul. No one will ever BE you or do your purpose work in the world like you! Do you know how powerful and special YOUR magic is? You are rare and can never be duplicated, ever! That is pure magic all by itself. Can you imagine what your life will be like when you embrace this powerful truth? You are rare, pure magic!

—Catrice M. Jackson

And just in case you forgot, the most powerful chess piece is the black queen! It's time to make your move, Sis. Go forth. Maximize your magic. Don't be hesitant about who you are. And be *Unf*ckablewith* about it too!

Writing Prompts to Rise from the Ashes

How have you been infected by Whiteness?

_____

_____

_____

_____

_____

_____

_____

_____

How does your anti-blackness show up?

_____

_____

_____

_____

_____

_____

_____

How have you become paralyzed by the White Gaze?

_____

_____

_____

_____

_____

_____

_____

How would you define your magic?

_____

_____

_____

_____

_____

_____

What does rising from the ashes look like for you?

_____

_____

_____

_____

_____

_____

_____

How will you use your magic to rise from your ashes?

_____

_____

_____

_____

_____

_____

_____

_____

_____

_____

How will you choose to NOT be hesitant about who you are?

_____

_____

_____

_____

_____

_____

_____

_____

_____

_____

_____

UNF*CKABLEWITH

SHONDA RHIMES

FASCINATING

"Ditch the dream and be a doer."

Shonda Rhimes

* * * * * * *

CHAPTER SIX

FASCINATING

Black people.

We are fascinating.

Just damn splendid! Right?

When we choose to sprinkle our magic onto things, they pop, sizzle, and ooze with flava! I love black people. Can't nobody do it like us. It's taken me years to get to this place of loving all different kinds of blackness and resisting the urge to be anti-black. I haven't mastered it, but I work hard every day to celebrate the beauty, power, strength, and genius of black folks, especially black women. As a people watcher, I often wonder what other black women are thinking and feeling as they move through the world. Especially my SisSTARS who got that *Unf*ckablewith* vibe! Bold and confident black women who navigate spaces totally unbothered and unmoved by the white gaze. Bloop! Black women are fascinating!

There are times when I wish I could read minds. Human behavior and psychology fascinate me. I don't consider myself to be much of a woo-woo kind of person, by which I mean someone who is deep into and well-versed in the spiritual realm. However, I do believe we are all born with innate spiritual abilities. I know enough about my zodiac sign (Scorpio), a smidge about the healing properties of crystals, and a dab about the spiritual gifts described in the Bible. That's it. I believe in prophecy and visions, as my grandmother and mother call them. I didn't think I was into tarot cards or palm readings, but an interesting experience I had with the latter may have changed my mind. I've also had many dreams in my lifetime that I knew had significant meanings. When that happens, I call my mother to help me translate them.

My mother helps me translate dreams because this is her spiritual gift. For as long as I can remember, my mother has been having visions and translating dreams. When I was younger, I thought it was weird and that she was exaggerating, but as I got older, I saw some of her dreams come to pass. Sometimes she would call me on the phone and say, "I need to tell this dream to someone so it will come to pass, or so God will show me a new vision about what's going to happen next." She was adamant that for either of these things to happen, she needed to tell the dream to at least three people. And she always did. Between my mother's visions, my dreams, and my palm-reading experience, let's just say I have several fascinating stories to tell you.

My first fascinating story took place not too long after I had my son in 1992. My mother told me she had a dream about my future husband. She described him as a tall, medium-brown-skinned man, and she said she would know him when she saw him, and it would be undeniable. She told me to look up Proverbs 18:22 in the Bible, which reads, *"He who finds a wife finds a good thing, And obtains favor from the Lord"* (New King James Version, Prov. 18:22). She told me to read the scripture and write the name "Ray" next to it.

At this point, I was convinced my mother's gift was real because I had seen too many of her visions come to pass. So I was obedient and wrote the name "Ray" in my Bible, but then I forgot about it. At that time, I wasn't necessarily looking for a husband, although I had not only grown tired of frivolous relationships with men, but also realized that my son's biological father was uninterested in being part of our family.

I went on with life as usual, but every now and then, when I was interested in a guy, I would have him meet my mother to see if she would say, "Yes, that's him!" (It wasn't as odd as it may sound because at the time I was living with her.) Like my mother, I was not a woman who dated or slept with many men. In fact, I can still count the men I've slept with on one hand, and I've been with one man, my husband, for twenty-five years. No shade on women who sleep with lots of men. It just wasn't in my nature. It wasn't my thing. In particular, I remember bringing two men to meet my mother. The first one was a friend of mine who came over to my mother's house to see me. He stayed for a little while, we hung out a bit, and then he left. And you know it. As soon as he left, I asked my mother, "Is that him?" Without hesitation she said, "No!"

After several months passed, a similar situation occurred with a second guy. And yep, the response was the same: "Nope, that's not him!" I have to admit that even though I knew my mother had the gift of "seeing the future," if you will, I was bored with the idea that my husband would just show up one day and my mother would say, "Yes, that's him." I mean, really, that sounds like some kind of fairy tale. After the second guy, I forgot about the whole husband thing and just went on living my life. And again, if I'm honest, I really did want a husband and a father for my son, but I wasn't going to keep playing the "is this him" game. Instead, I decided he would show up when he was meant to show up.

In the fall of 1993, I was out at the club with my girlfriends. At one point, I got up from the table to go use the bathroom. On my way there, I passed a group of men, and this one guy was just staring and smiling at me like he knew me. When I walked past him again on the way back to my table, he did the same thing. It seemed peculiar, so I told my girlfriends about it. We laughed and that was it.

The next weekend, I was at a different club and saw my friend Calvin there. I went up to him and asked what he was drinking. We had this thing where one weekend he would buy my drinks, and the next weekend, I would buy his. We were good friends and we were cool like that. I was so uninterested in men at the time that I didn't even notice that standing next to Calvin was the same peculiar guy who had been staring at me at the other club the weekend before.

This guy with Calvin said to me, "You buying drinks tonight?" I said, "Not for you, I don't even know you." I recognized him then because he was standing there with that same silly grin he'd had when I'd seen him the previous weekend. I went to the bar, bought Calvin a drink, went back to sit with my friends, and forgot about the guy with the big grin. But the next couple of times I went out with my girlfriends, I saw him again, and each time he would stare and smile at me. One weekend, I mustered up the courage to approach him and start a conversation. I asked him why he was always staring and grinning at me. He didn't say much, just laughed. We engaged in small talk, and he eventually asked for my phone number. I gave it to him.

I told him that the following weekend was my birthday, and that he should come to my party and bring some friends. He did. We all danced and had a great time, except for him; turns out he wasn't a dancer. Over the next month or so we talked on the phone and occasionally saw each other. I was beginning to like him a bit more. I was still living with my mother at that time, and one day she hollered upstairs, "Nan, somebody is here to see you." I told her to send them up. I was watching television and playing with my one-year-old son, so I didn't really notice there was a brief delay before the person came upstairs. When I looked up and saw who it was, I thought, *Oh my gosh!* It was the grinning guy I'd been hanging out with and getting to know.

I was shocked for two reasons. First, I wondered how he knew where I lived, and second, I wondered why he was showing up unannounced. It was awkward, to say the least. I lived in a small town and everyone (the black folks, at least) knew me, and many knew where I lived. He came into my room and asked if he could sit on the bed, and I said yes. He said, "Is this your son?" I said it was and told him my son's name. He asked if he could hold him. In my mind I was thinking, *What the hell you want to hold my son for, I don't know you like that!* But I said yes and watched everything he did while he was holding my son. Everything. Seriously! You've got to watch how people engage with your children because there are some sick folks out there. What struck me was that the guy held my son like he knew him. He held my son like he was his own. Nothing weird or strange, but I could tell the guy liked kids, and that he was genuinely interested in my son and not just in me.

After he left, you KNOW I had to go ask my mama if he was the one. I couldn't wait until he left so I could get the scoop from her. After I let him out and closed the door, I went back into the living room, sat down with a big grin on my face, and said, "So, what do you think?" She acted like she didn't hear me. She smiled. She was really dragging it out, and I couldn't stand the anticipation. Finally, she said, "Yes, he's the one." I was smiling inside and trying to hold back my outward smile. I couldn't believe it. I wanted to believe it, but how could she really know? So I asked her. She said, "Did you notice he didn't come upstairs right after getting here?" I said I did. She said, "I was trying to capture enough time with him so God could speak to me, so I could feel who he was in my spirit."

She told me more things that I no longer remember. But then she said I should get my Bible and look at what I had written in it. I went upstairs, got the Bible, found the scripture, and read what she told me months ago. It was damn near exact. He looked like she said he would look. He behaved like she said he would behave, and although his name wasn't Ray, it was pretty darn close. His name is Roy. This just fascinates me! Long story short, here we are twenty-five years later, still married, and still doing the work to stay married. My mama was right. She often is, and I believe in her gift of seeing the future. I think I may have this gift too, but I don't want it, so I avoid listening to this particular kind of spiritual insight most of the time.

I had another fascinating story occur in 1995. That year, I had a horrible dream that I was upstairs in my grandmother's house, and I was trying to get away from some kind of danger. She lived in a big two-story house with twenty-plus stairs leading to the second floor. I don't know why exactly, but I always thought it was creepy going up and down those stairs. Maybe because only my grandparents lived in the house, and because my stingy grandfather would have a fit if we left lights on in rooms that no one was in, so the house and stairway were often dark and quiet. As I was trying to run down the stairs in my dream, I realized when I took the first step down that the rest of the staircase had turned into murky water.

I kept trying to get down the stairs to get away from the invisible danger, but I couldn't run because the water was almost knee deep and it seemed heavy and resistant. Somehow I eventually made my way to the bottom of the stairs. When I got to the French doors leading into the living room, I shut the door, and was free from whatever was chasing me. That was all I remembered from the dream, but I knew it had a profound meaning. I knew it was a vision. God was trying to warn me about something, but I didn't know how to translate it. The next day I called my mom and told her the dream. She said I was in danger and that God was trying to warn me to stay away from something that meant me no good.

My mother told me I was going to experience some kind of pain if I returned to something that God had said to walk away from. I had no idea what that could be or what she was talking about. For the first few days after the dream, I remained vigilant, trying to make sure I didn't do something that would be dangerous to me. But after a few weeks, I forgot about the dream. Then one day, I decided I was going rejoin the church I had left a few years before. I had left the church along with some other members when the pastor got caught up in some kind of adultery scandal. At one time it had been a thriving church, and I had been an active member, but with so many leaving it was starting to crumble. I decided to go back to the church and recommit to the choir, so on this day, I was going to choir rehearsal.

It was the first time I was visiting the new church location. It was a big, old building, and it was two or three stories tall. One of the deacons of the church took us on a tour. After the tour, as I was walking down a narrow staircase to return to the sanctuary, I missed a step and twisted my left ankle. The pain was excruciating, but I finally made it to the bottom of the stairs. That's when I realized I couldn't walk on my left leg at all. I was screaming and in so much pain that my husband plus two or three other men had to help me get into my car. I thought my ankle was broken, but it was a severe strain. After going to the hospital, I still couldn't walk. I knew I wasn't going to be able to take care of myself and my son while my husband worked, so I went to stay at my mother's house. The sprain was so bad that my ankle was achy and bruised for about three months.

This dream I shared with you was a vision. God was warning me to not go back to something that was going to be dangerous to me for reasons I did not know. My mother warned me. I was warned. I believe now—partly because I didn't know how to translate the message, and partly because I didn't truly believe it—that God had created a situation where I literally couldn't return to the church. This may sound strange, but I believe it to be true. My gut knows it's the truth even though I can't fully explain it. I never did return to the church, and yes, all hell broke loose there and I'm glad I wasn't involved. Occasionally, I still have vivid and profound dreams, and often they are scary and wake me up. I don't always know what they mean. Most times I don't want to know, but I always call my mama for translation, and what she says always comes to pass.

These types of spiritual gifts fascinate me, and as the previous story illustrates, I have a visionary gift similar to my mother's. But if I'm honest, I'm afraid of truly accessing the power of these gifts. I really don't want to know, so I avoid knowing if possible. How about you? Do you know what your spiritual gifts are? Do you embrace them or avoid them? How are you using your spiritual gifts to activate your magic and/or be of service to others? This is one spiritual gift I choose not to embrace. I'm not sure if I am "suffering" any consequences because of my refusal to embrace it. However, I choose to let others with this gift shine in their genius. I believe in this power, but I don't want it for myself.

Now, let me share one more fascinating story with you. In 2015, I was a speaker at a travel conference in California. I had just finished my presentation, and I was taking a break and selling books at my vendor booth. When the crowd died down, I decided to walk around and visit some of the other booths. I remembered seeing a woman and man who were doing hand massages at the end of the hall, so I decided to go get one. As I approached their table, I saw the woman. I thought she might be Indian, and I found out later she was. I preferred having her do my hand massage over the white man, who looked suspicious and out of place. His eyes were the brightest blue I'd ever seen, and he appeared to be kind of zoned out. You know, kind of like his body was there, but his mind was somewhere else.

As I approached their table, the Indian woman jumped like she had seen a ghost. I clearly saw her. Her reaction struck me, but not as much as what happened next. She gazed at me for a moment, and then began to quickly massage the hand of her white woman customer. The Indian woman seemed to be hurrying the white woman along by rushing through her massage, even though she had just started a few minutes earlier. I stood and waited. I thought to myself, *I don't want her rushing my massage like that.* For a split second I considered the white guy, but then decided, *Nah, he's weird.*

Finally, the Indian woman smiled like a Chessa cat (Cheshire cat, but that's the way my Gran used to say it) and said, "Come, sit down." I took a seat and looked at her. Her eyes were shining like diamonds, her hair was thick, black, and lustrous, and her energy was pulsating with excitement. She was beautiful.

She grabbed my left hand and began massaging one spot on my palm. Slowly and rhythmically she rubbed the spot between my pointer and middle finger. I was like, *Wait a damn minute, isn't she going to use some fancy massage oil or anything?* This was the strangest hand massage ever. The woman kept gazing at me. It was like she was reading me. Turns out, she was.

She asked me why I was at the conference, and I told her I had just finished speaking. She asked what I spoke about, and I said

I had talked about monetizing your brand. Still she gazed. Still she rubbed the same damn spot on my palm. Then she scoffed! "Branding," she said. "That's not your real message."

Shocked and intrigued by her comment, I said, "Oh really, how do you know?"

"Because you have another message inside of you that you should be speaking about."

Sis, listen... I was ready to get up out that damn chair and walk away, okay? No, this woman did NOT just tell me she knows more about my message than I do! But I stayed seated because I was wary and fascinated at the same time. I truly wanted to hear what she had to say.

She leaned toward me. "Branding and marketing are not your message. They are not what you are here to do." Before I could answer, she said, "You have another message, don't you?"

I felt like the wind had been knocked out of me. This was not your ordinary hand massage. *This woman is reading my palm! Shit! What the hell?* That's what I was thinking. And I was afraid, because I had never willingly allowed anyone to read my palms before. Listen... my grandmother and mama taught me to be leery of "those" kinds of folks. And I was. I wanted to get up so bad, but she had a tight grip on my hand.

Curious and cautious, I told her I had another message that longed to be spoken, but I was unsure how to speak it and afraid of the repercussions of doing so. I shared that my soul had been begging me for years to talk about racism, white supremacy, and the racial violence that white women commit against black women. I told her I knew this was my purpose and calling, and I was choosing to run from it because it's scary, difficult, and controversial.

She said, "Don't be afraid, Catrice. God gave you this message. This is your work to do." And out of the blue she jumped again.

Startled! She was gazing over my head and still rubbing the same spot on my palm.

That's it! This shit is weird, and I feel uncomfortable, I thought. Out loud, I said, "Thank you for the massage, but I better get back to the conference."

She said, "No, please stay. There is more I want to share."

"Listen," I said, "this is the second time I've seen you have a startled response, what is that all about?"

"Catrice, right as I was telling you to not be afraid, I saw an image of you sitting on a CNN panel as an expert on race relations." She continued, "Catrice, the world is waiting for you to speak this message. The world needs this message. This is your message. You're going to be famous one day for this message."

Oh my gosh! What did this woman just say to me? CNN? Expert? Famous!

She said, "Catrice, I need you to be obedient. Go home and stop talking about branding. That is not your purpose or your destiny. God has great plans for you, don't be afraid. Believe me."

My mind was blown. I could feel her grip soften and she slowly released my hands. Smiling bright and eyes glistening, she said, "Trust your message, Catrice. Do it now and don't be afraid."

My eyes welled with tears. As freaking strange as this moment was, I knew she was right. Every cell in my body was saying *yes!* I felt warm, comforted, and affirmed. Now that I was free to leave, I wanted to stay. I wanted to hear more, and I had one more question for her. I said, "Hey, I noticed when I walked up to your table that you seemed startled then too, and you were rushing that woman out of your seat. Why?"

"Catrice, do you know how powerful you are? I felt your energy before I saw your face, and when you stood before me, your energy was so breathtaking, I knew I had to touch you." She went on to say that my energy is like Oprah energy: powerful and legendary. She encouraged me one final time to be obedient to the call on my life.

For a brief moment, I could not move my feet. What do you do when someone tells you something profound and prophetic like that? Every time I travel somewhere, I know there is ONE lesson or message I am to receive. On that California trip, the message to obey my true calling was it.

I walked back to my table. Gathered my things. Boxed up my books and took them back up to my hotel room. I chose to be immediately obedient. My session with the Indian woman had shaken me and woken me up. I had never experienced anything like it before. I was scared, excited, and anxious to get home. I had no idea how I was going to manifest this message, but I said yes to my soul.

When I got home, I started dismantling everything I had created as the BOSSLady of Branding. The next day, I made an announcement on Facebook that I would no longer be offering branding and marketing services, and I shared what had happened while I was in California. This call to action happened in March of 2015. By October of 2015, I had completed my first anti-racism, racial justice book called *Antagonists, Advocates and Allies*. And I have never looked back. What a fascinating experience!

I may not ever get another palm reading, but people have special spiritual gifts that intrigue me. Even with my limited knowledge about such things, I know that in addition to my prophetic dreams, I possess clairsentience and claircognizance. I won't go into detail about these, but I will say I am a masterful reader and sensor of energy, and I tend to just know things with clarity and conviction. I can smell a lie a mile away. I can tell instantly whether someone is trustworthy or not. I can pick up on another person's energy despite what their words say. My intuition is sharp, unfailing, and powerful. Some people have called me a seer and an oracle. I can own the seer part, but oracle, that's a bit too much for my humbleness to handle. Authenticity is so important to me. And at the end of the day, what matters most is that I am true to myself, that I love and embrace every part of who I am, and that I show up as who I say I am.

All in all, though, I wish I could read people's minds. Especially the minds of black women. I would love to be able to tap into and experience the thoughts of the great black women (and men) who came before me and of those living today. As I do this racial justice work, I often wonder what Harriet Tubman, Fannie Lou Hamer, or Rosa Parks were thinking when they put their bodies on the line for justice and fought for the liberation of black people. And sometimes I wish they could speak to me directly to guide me on my journey of being a voice for black people. At least I sense their energy with me as I walk this difficult and emotional path.

I wish I could hear the thoughts of my great-grandmother Rachel, who was a slave. I wish I could hear the thoughts of my grandmother, who wasn't taught to read, but who was a mighty spiritual warrior and lover of God. I wish I could hear the thoughts of my mother, who had to endure the violent Jim Crow Era. I wish I could hear the voices and thoughts of all the black folks who resisted white supremacy and bondage, of those who persisted and rebelled against the horrific system trying to kill them, and of those who died trying.

Sometimes I wonder if I could stand to hear what my ancestors would tell me about their life experiences. I know I would feel anger, maybe even rage. I'm sure I would weep and maybe even wail empathetic tears. But I wonder if my body could literally tolerate the stories of pain, struggle, and horror. In December of 2017, I visited the Whitney Plantation in Louisiana for the first time with my husband. I'd longed to experience a plantation for the past twenty years and kept putting it off for various reasons. One of those reasons was that I truly did not want to face the barbaric legacy of whiteness lingering in the blood-soaked soil where black people, my people, had been treated worse than animals. Yet I went, because my soul wouldn't let me rest until I faced the truth of evil personified. I needed to see the land of terror with my own eyes.

As soon as my feet touched the sacred ground leading up to the church, the first stop on the tour, chills ran through me. I felt like I had just stepped out of a time machine that had taken me back to my roots. I don't know if any of my folks were enslaved on that plantation. It didn't matter who the captives were. They were *my* people. For two hours, I walked the plantation grounds, observing remnants of inhumane circumstances and traces of treachery. I vacillated between moments of anger and despair. And every now and then, between moments of joy and hope. Rage erupted as I viewed the cement plaques listing countless names of enslaved Africans. I felt rage after entering the destitute slave quarters, and I felt it again when I looked out the back window up at the big house.

The tour guide said that two or three families would occupy one dilapidated shack, which means up to fifteen people were crammed into a two-room prison. I felt rage watching white folks tour the grounds while talking too damn much, taking up space, taking pictures, and consuming most of the conversation with the tour guide. Like, why the f*ck were they even there? I was pissed. I made my pissed-offedness obvious. I took up extra space, as much as I could. I refused to move out of white folks' way. I moved to the front of the tour line. I took my time observing things, and I purposely made white folks wait their turn. I vocalized whatever the f*ck I was feeling and cared less what the white folks thought.

Close to the end of the tour, we were guided to the front of the big house. As I turned the corner from the back of the building, scenes from the movie 12 Years A Slave flooded my mind. And for a moment, as I approached the end of the long walkway leading up to the big house, I felt like I was a character in that movie. It was exactly how I imagined it would be. A shaded, cobblestone-like walkway tucked under enormous trees with stout trunks at least six or seven feet wide. Beautifully eerie trees, with twisted branches that seemed to stretch as long as a city block, perfectly entangled to create a whimsical web of deception and deceit.

Those trees were fascinating! I was so deeply enchanted by them that I veered off from the crowd and took a slow stroll down the cobblestone walkway by myself. The trees were stunning works of art. Every imperfect branch was perfectly intertwined with other branches to create a striking canopy covering the walkway. I was completely captivated by those trees. They enveloped me, and it felt like they all gathered around me to comfort my pain. In solitude, I was mesmerized by their magnificence. I paused for a moment and asked my ancestors to speak to me. I needed to hear their voices. And in the soft whistling of the wind, I heard my ancestors speak. Standing motionless and alone in the middle of the trees, I heard breathtaking ancestral whispers of comfort and affirmation. This was one of my few glimpses of joy on this journey.

I heard my ancestors in the wind. I believe I heard my great-grandmother Rachel. Sometimes I heard delicate whispers, and other times I heard wailing murmurs. I heard the voices clearly say, "Don't be afraid, we are with you." And I heard them say, "Carry the torch, go forth, and be brave." Every time I heard them speak, I wept.

I cried tears of pain, despair, and joy.

I gasped. I didn't care who was watching.

I didn't hide my tears. I wept. And wept some more.

Expelling animosity and anguish without apology.

Inhaling fresh fuel and insight for my journey ahead.

There was healing in the trees.

I was reaffirmed and renewed.

My spirit was alchemized.

I was nourished.

Unleashing cathartic cries alone with the trees cleansed my soul and revitalized my passion to fight for the justice and liberation of black people. I will never forget those trees. My moment under the captivating canopy, hearing my ancestors speak—that was a monumental and meaningful experience.

I still don't know how I would respond to hearing the horrific stories of my ancestors. But I have to believe I am resilient enough to hold space and bear witness. And I believe my ancestors would also share glimpses of joy and triumph. I know I am able and willing to hear those messages. The possibility intrigues me. How about you? Do you long to hear the voices and stories of your ancestors? What would you like them to tell you? Do you believe you'd be able to hold space and bear witness to their stories of pain and struggle? I feel pretty confident in saying that the struggles our black women ancestors faced in their lives were much more challenging than those we experience today. Their will to fight, survive, and thrive lives within us.

* * * * * * * *

I want to circle back to my story about the palm reader in California. She asked me a pivotal question, one I have for you: *Do you know how powerful you are?* And if you're struggling with seeing yourself as powerful, do you know how capable, clever, and dynamic you are? I imagine that the black women I spoke of in the first paragraph of this chapter, my SisSTARS who are *Unf*ckablewith,* know their power. It takes confidence and courage to move through the world unbothered and unapologetic. Especially when society deems everything about your blackness to be undesirable, unacceptable, and intolerable. A powerful black woman is a threat to everyone, because we're not supposed to exist for our own edification and agency. I'm fascinated by black women who embody, own, and express their melanin magic.

One of those fascinating black women is Shonda Rhimes! A television writer and producer, author, and single mother of three daughters, she fascinates the world through her work and through her company Shondaland. She is the mastermind behind the television shows *Grey's Anatomy, Scandal,* and *How to Get Away with Murder* (my favorite show). Her work is absolutely brilliant. It's spellbinding. Her creativity and storytelling are mesmerizing and phenomenal. Shonda has definitely tapped into her genius and maximizes her innate gifts to entertain the world. She is one example of a black woman who has unleashed her fascinating to not only create the life she desires, but also to entertain the world.

One thing I love about Shonda is her unflinching belief that you can make your dreams a reality. At one point, before she became the powerhouse she is today, she lived in her sister's basement. She never stopped believing and striving toward her dreams while depending on someone else for shelter. I imagine there were folks who didn't believe Shonda would be who she is today. I imagine they thought she was a failure because she had to live with her sister. Maybe you're dependent on other folks for your basic needs too. That doesn't mean you should stop dreaming. You're not a failure. I had to live with my mother during many moments of transition, and I kept on dreaming and working to actualize my dreams. You can too.

Black women's ability to continuously rise from the ashes of grief, pain, and failure is mind-blowing, yet oh-so-believable. Whatever you may be dealing with or going through right now, I know you have the ability to regenerate and rise again. I also believe that your fascinating serves as a propellent in your ascent. What I mean by "your fascinating" are the qualities and characteristics that make you fascinating! It's your *Unf*ckablewith* vibe. It's your boldness and confidence. It's how you navigate spaces totally unbothered and unmoved by the white gaze. Anyone's gaze, for that matter! If you want to rise into your black woman badassery, Sis, find *your fascinating* and unleash that shit without apology.

Writing Prompts to Rise from the Ashes

What do you find fascinating about black women?

_____

_____

_____

_____

_____

_____

_____

_____

How would you define your fascinating?

_____

_____

_____

_____

_____

_____

_____

_____

What are your spiritual gifts, and how do you use them to embody your black woman badassery?

_____

_____

_____

_____

_____

_____

How can you use your fascinating to rise from your ashes?

_____

_____

_____

_____

_____

Are you commanding respect and taking up the space that you rightfully deserve?

_____

_____

_____

_____

_____

When you move through the world, what kind of energy do you exude or want to exude?

_____

_____

_____

_____

_____

_____

_____

_____

_____

_____

What do you love about your blackness, and how can you embody, own, and express it so you feel alive?

_____

_____

_____

_____

_____

_____

_____

_____

ASSATA SHAKUR

DARING

"Revolution is about change, and the first place
the change begins is in yourself."

Assata Shakur

* * * * * * *

CHAPTER SEVEN

DARING

The older white man sat in the back of the room with his arms folded. He stared unabashedly at just about every woman who spoke that day. He was trying to keep a low profile, but I spotted him before the anti-racism workshop began, and I knew to keep an eye on him. For the longest time, he didn't say a word.

I'm the kind of presenter who moves around the room when I speak or teach. Doing so helps me feel the energy of the space and connect with the souls sitting in the seats. Shortly after the presentation began, I moved to the back of the room to better hear a black woman who had volunteered to share her truth. She was speaking about an experience where she had been shut down and silenced by a white person. I could sense she was feeling something deep and was getting emotional. When she finished, I validated her by reframing and clarifying what she said to create a powerful teaching moment for the white folks in the workshop.

Apparently, the white man didn't like what I said, because he aggressively interrupted me and the black woman while we were talking. He boldly disagreed with me and offered his own unsolicited comments.

Say what? Aww, hell to the no! I moved toward him and said, "This is what you will NOT do in this space. You will NOT speak over black women, you will NOT disrespect the black woman who owns this space, and you will NOT try to discredit me, a black woman, in our own damn black space!"

The white man continued to interject and disrupt the workshop. He was refusing to back down and respect the black women in the room.

"You will sit down, be quiet, and stop this violent behavior, or you will leave," I told him. The room of mostly white folks was frozen. They were not dismayed by his outlandish, sexist, and racist behavior, but by the fact that I, a black woman, dared to unapologetically hold this white man accountable for his aggressive behavior.

The man kept on pushing the issue by interrupting and taking up space. I asked the room, "Will somebody go get Michael? Because we are not playing up in here with this man!" Michael (not the black man's real name) is the husband of the black woman I was co-facilitating the workshop with.

"I'll be good. I'll be quiet," the white man said.

With fire in my eyes and thunder in my voice, I said, *"Oh! Now we gonna get some act right up in here!"* When I sent for Michael, the white man knew I was serious. Serious as a heart attack. He sat in the workshop for the duration of the presentation and didn't say another damn word. Not one. And I wish he would have!

Listen. There were at least three other white men and two black men in the room. Not one of them stood up or spoke up to protect the black women in the room. The workshop was filled with predominantly white women. And you know not one of THEM was brave enough to say anything. Beckys love to put their foot on our throats, but most ain't got the backbone to stand up to white men, their real oppressors.

How dare I boldly confront this white man on his racial violence? That was the sentiment on the faces of some of the white folks in the room. How dare I not confront him? It is my right and duty to confront anyone who is disrespectful in my spaces, and to confront anyone who is disrespectful to me or other black women. This act of daringness, one that black women must do on the regular, is both a risk and a necessity. History and the current state of affairs tells black women what happens when we confront white male terrorism. Yes, I call it terrorism, because it sure the hell isn't supremacy.

When black women dare to speak up for ourselves, we are seen as angry and intimidating. When we dare to demand respect, we are perceived as threatening, and are at risk for emotional and physical harm. When black women defy the expectation to shut up and stay in our place, we are in danger. Always. Yet if we don't dare to be daring, we know we are dying inside.

Dying from the betrayal of self.

Dying from conformity and cowardice.

Dying from tolerating disrespect.

Dying from allowing ourselves to be disregarded, disdained, and dehumanized.

If we do not defend ourselves and demand respect, who will? Everyone comes for black women, including other black women. And it's a hard truth, but not all black men dare to defend us. Essentially, we're all we've got. Every day we take spontaneous and calculated risks to quantify our value, defend our humanity, and honor our integrity, so we can literally survive and emotionally thrive. And when we do, we are blackballed, blacklisted, and blacked out. When we dare to honor our value, we are chastised, accused, ignored, reported, written up, fired, shunned, silenced, verbally abused, and sometimes physically attacked. We are damned if we do and damned if we don't. So I choose to speak up and daringly defend my humanity. Zora Neale Hurston was right when she said, "If you are silent about your pain, they'll kill you and say you enjoyed it." And not only that you enjoyed it—they'll say you asked for it. They'll say you caused your own punishment. They'll blame you even in death.

I know it is maddening and exhausting to be constantly defensive, and I also know not every attack needs to be dealt with directly for you to have peace and to experience joy. But what's the alternative? If you stand up and speak up for yourself, you exert tremendous emotional energy and waste your precious life source. If you choose to stay silent, they'll kill you. If you choose to speak up, you put yourself at risk. If you choose to stay silent, you teach people how to treat you. If you choose to speak up, you may lose people and things that matter to you. If you choose to stay silent, you betray your honor. Either way, you die inside. The only conclusion I can draw is that we must do both, and we must choose which response is appropriate in the moment, according to our need for peace and our desire to thrive. The dichotomy is that we must not let whiteness kill us, and we must not kill ourselves.

All the shit that black folks endure reminds me of James Baldwin's quote: "To be a negro in this country and to be relatively conscious is to be in a rage almost all the time." What becomes of someone who is in a rage almost all the time? What does that rage do to the bodies, minds, and souls of black folks? It's killing us. I can't imagine how often we emotionally die inside every day and what toll those deaths take on us over a lifetime. The attacks on us are endless and relentless. And even when we are not in the direct line of fire, the residual effects of these attacks attach to us like leeches and suck the life out of us. We emotionally die from:

Invalidation.

Insults.

Assaults.

Profiling.

Prejudice.

Exclusion.

Discrimination.

Alienation.

Marginalization.

Criminalization.

White folks' imagination.

Fetishization.

Infantilization.

These are the daggers we face that cause us to bleed. This is how society kills us emotionally. Slowly. Strategically. Systematically and relentlessly. This is why black women rage. And our rage is most often directed inward and onto those who look like us. We hurt ourselves and each other disproportionately. The way in which we rage is vast and destructive, and it puts us in a perpetual state of fight, flight, and freeze. We fight the systems, we fight ourselves, and we fight each other. By "fight," I mean we resist violence, react to violence, and enact violence. And "violence" is the appropriate term to use in this context because any act against oneself or others that causes harm or trauma is abuse, and abuse is violence.

Existing in a constant state of stress creates the perfect breeding ground for disease, dysfunction, and depression. It's important to state that depression is rage (anger) turned inward. Disease, dysfunction, and depression stresses the body. Stress attacks and compromises our immune system, our cognition, and our emotional resiliency. Our body's ability to fight off viruses decreases under stress and our mental agility is stifled. Damn, it seems like it is a lose-lose situation for black women. If you don't fight back against racial stress, it will win. If you flee from or avoid confronting racial stress, it will compound and eventually affect you. If you freeze and become paralyzed by racial stress, it will consume you. And if you're not conscious, racial stress will cause you to burn. Any of these natural responses to racial stress is a death trap and results in creating the ashes in your life. So either you let the fire devour you, or you become the fire.

It's important for me to acknowledge that your rage is justified. And if you need to or choose to become the fire, I will blaze with you. Be the fire. Burn the shit that tries to kill you to the ground. Just don't let the fire consume you. It is possible to turn black pain into black power. This is how you rise from the ashes into your black woman badassery. This is how you become *Unf*ckablewith*. There may be times when the appropriate response to an attack is to fight, flee, or freeze. Are there other alternatives? The only alternative I see is you must learn to get free and live free. And I realize doing so is easier said than done. Until we begin to liberate ourselves and get free, we will continue to rage and wage war against ourselves. Freedom is our best choice. Freedom is our only choice. So how do we get free? And what does "free" mean to you?

According to livescience.com, "[F]reedom is the power or right to act, speak, or think as one wants without hindrance or restraint." Based on this definition, are you free? You have the inherent power to act, speak, or think as you want, but can you do so without hindrance or restraint? Who or what controls your ability to do so? Who or what tries to obstruct your inherent power to act, speak, or think as you choose? I think we can agree that systems of oppression and power put limits on our freedom, and they work to obstruct our autonomy. As women, we know systems and practices of patriarchy serve to silence and marginalize us. As black women, we know there are also systems and practices of whiteness that serve to keep us in our "place," to oppress us, and to remain in control.

Another issue for black people is that we are in a constant state of double-consciousness. Even those of us who work daily to live free. Even when we believe we are *Unf*ckablewith* down in our bones, society comes along and tells us we're not, and it puts poison in our path to try to kill us. In his book *The Souls of Black Folk*, W.E.B. Du Bois says, "It is a peculiar sensation, this double-consciousness, this sense of always looking at one's self through the eyes of others, of measuring one's soul by the tape of a world that looks on in amused contempt and pity." I translate this to mean we see ourselves and determine our value and worth according to the white gaze, which doesn't see our value and worth. Ain't that some delusional shit? And delusion it is. It's delusional because we have centuries of facts, incidents, documentation, and evidence illustrating how white folks view us. White terrorism still reigns, but we still don't believe what collective whiteness thinks about us, even though the proof stares us in the face. Proof that is at least four hundred years old and counting.

This double-consciousness is a false belief that is maintained despite indisputable evidence to the contrary, and it creates internal conflict. We can believe we are beautiful, intelligent, valuable, and deserving, yet every day we must face the rules, standards, and laws that tell us we are ugly, stupid, and worthless. Double-consciousness can lead to not knowing yourself, minimizing your magic, and downplaying your worth, and it can lead to confusion, sadness, bitterness, anxiety, depression, self-hate, and yes, anti-blackness. It's self-deprecating to consciously or unconsciously use the mark and proximity of whiteness to measure your value and worth. Operating in a state of double-consciousness will not get you free. The white gaze is one hell of a drug. And a lot of black folks are strung out. Are you addicted to the white gaze? What are you going to do so the white gaze does not consume you or dictate how you show up in the world?

Seeking, craving, and adhering to the white gaze, and using the white gaze as a tool to measure our value and worth, are behaviors that fall within the realm of Stockholm syndrome. Stockholm syndrome is a psychological response in which a captive begins to identify closely with their captor, as well as the captor's agenda and demands. At the heart of this syndrome is the desire to survive a threatening situation. Someone who is being held against their will, especially if they are in fear of dying, will work to appease their captor. If their life is spared, they will develop deep gratitude for the captor's grace. This gratitude begins to transform into fondness and admiration. And the longer the prisoner is held, the deeper and more emotionally entrenched this fondness and admiration becomes. They even start feeling protective of their oppressor. Sound familiar? Are you caping for white folks?

It takes only a few days of captivity for Stockholm syndrome to manifest. Black folks have been "captive" in so many ways for centuries that it's no wonder many of us have Stockholm syndrome tendencies. You have no idea how many black women I've met who go hard for white women, prop them up, glorify them, defend them, and fight to protect their white "friend." Black women who so desperately want to be accepted and valued by whiteness they will throw other black women under the bus. I've encountered black women who have cut me in the dark as a strategy to gain access to white women I'm connected to. And other black women have taken to social media to bash and trash my work and my credibility as a strategy to showcase their own work designed for white folks. To attract the white gaze, they were willing to kill me with their words.

I may be preaching to the choir as it relates to the weapons black women use against each other, and perhaps you've been wounded by a few black daggers in your life too. I know I've drawn my weapons in the past, and I still have to disarm myself if I truly want to be free. What weapons are you wielding against your black sisters? Why are you trying to wound them? I'm getting better at going to bat for black women even when they don't go hard for me. I'm also learning how to discern when my fellow sisters are not in a space of reciprocity, when they don't know how to return the love and support. Sure, it stings, and I may even feel hurt or angry temporarily. But I'm learning to release my sisters with love, because I know they are going through their own search for truth and are on their own path to liberation.

So back to this moment in the workshop with the white guy. There was no way in hell I was going to stand by and allow him to harm the black women in the room. I didn't react with fight, flight, or freeze. Instead, I dared to respond with freedom. My inherent right to stand up for black women. My inherent right to defy his weapons of whiteness. My inherent right to protect myself and the black women I love. Had I stayed quiet, I would have done what Zora Neale Hurston talks about: I would have been silent about my pain and allowed him to kill us. I would have allowed him to leave the workshop feeling boastful about how we enjoyed his attempted murder of us, and he would have blamed us for our emotional death. I chose to be and act free in that moment despite the consequences I might face. I chose to rise from the ashes of his attack into my black woman badassery!

* * * * * * *

Zora's truth about the consequences of us staying silent about our pain registers so intensely for me now. Had I heard her quote twenty years ago, I wouldn't have understood it, and I might have even rejected it. Back then, I was indoctrinated into the false belief that obtaining and maintaining the white gaze for personal evolution was the formula for success. I look back on my life and vividly see how I used (or attempted to use) this formula to not only get ahead, but also to get past my own people. Black people. And while looking in my rear-view mirror at them as I excelled, I minimized their struggle and mocked their ignorance of this fictitious formula. I also see the ways in which I allowed white folks to kill me, blame me, and lie and say I enjoyed it. I would keep my mouth shut to keep the white peace. I would bite my tongue instead of telling white folks off. I would ignore insults and assaults to keep my job. I would shuck and jive to make white folks comfortable while my integrity was battered, and I died inside.

The constant struggle of walking the fine line of allowing abuse and abusing yourself to survive the white gaze is emotionally terrorizing. Combine that with the terror we cause in other black folks' lives as a result of internalized oppression and anti blackness, and it's a psychological pit of hell. One thing you must understand: there is one source for this psychological warfare, and that is the infection of whiteness. A deadly virus that is relentless in emotionally killing not only its source, but also everyone else it latches onto. It may take centuries for this virus, this lethal infection, to die off. But we cannot wait for it to expire on its own. Personal, intentional, and direct action must be taken daily to not only rid yourself of it, but also to protect yourself from the exacerbation and transmission of it. James Baldwin says that after so many daily attacks of whiteness against your black spirit, you begin to believe what they say is true. Consciously and unconsciously. And when you internalize their lies as truth, you become your own accomplice in your murder. Damn, that's deeply disturbing and true.

At this point in my life, I'm undeniably clear that I choose to escape this obscene and obstructive oblivion of whiteness. Truth is, I can't think of one benevolent attribute of whiteness. In this case I'm not talking about white people but whiteness itself, the fallacy of this man-made construct that serves only to invade, steal, kill, conquer, and oppress. And when you or I allow this fallacy to thrive within us, then on some conscious or unconscious level, we use the callousness of this construct to kill not only ourselves, but also each other. I believe part of our most important personal work is to work within ourselves to escape this obscenity. To escape and liberate ourselves from the nastiness, lasciviousness, and unwholesomeness of whiteness and every shade of it. It's crude. It's vulgar. It's degenerate. It's not who we are. This work, this personal liberation work to free ourselves from the white gaze and all its expectations and demands, is the revolution. Our revolution. This is the work for black freedom and liberation.

Angela Davis was right to use "freedom is a constant struggle" as the title of her instructive book. We must always be daring in our quest for freedom and liberation. When black folks say the revolution will not be televised, they are so right, because the revolution begins inside of each of us. Inside of you! I am not completely free. I'm still infected. I'm still revolutionizing myself. My freedom is still a struggle. I don't have all the answers, and I'm still on my own personal journey of liberation. The one thing I know for sure while on this journey is that I choose—I dare!—to be consciously *Unf*ckablewith*. I am perfectly and imperfectly navigating my life, my revolution, my Beautiful Struggle. I am the revolution. You are the revolution.

When I think of daring black women, I think of Assata Shakur. In 1977, she was convicted of murdering a state trooper despite forensic evidence that supported her claims that she didn't kill him. Two years later, she escaped from a maximum security prison for women in New Jersey and fled to Cuba. She has been living there in exile since her escape. To this day, Assata Shakur is one of the FBI's Most Wanted "Terrorists." Wow! Can you even imagine what kind of bravery and mental fortitude it took to not only escape a maximum security prison, but also to flee one of the most powerful countries in the world? As daring as I believe I am, I am not sure I would have been able to do that. But Assata did. She did it because she believed in her innocence and in her right to freedom. How far are you willing to go to be free? What are you daring enough to do for your liberation? Assata is undoubtedly a revolutionary; are you?

Unf*ckablewith black women are the revolution and they will lead it. And remember, it's your *Unf*ckablewith* boldness and confidence that will help you defy the weapons used against you. I offer you some Weapons for Winning in the back of this book. These weapons or strategies come from my book *The Becky Code*. Use them to activate your *Unf*ckablewith!* You must be totally unbothered and unmoved by the white gaze. Anyone's gaze for that matter! If you want to rise into your black woman badassery, Sis, find your daring and unleash that shit without apology, too! Freedom is not going to be given to us; we must take it. Freedom is our right, and it is our duty to fight for it. Not only for ourselves, but also for each other. If the black women before us had not been daring enough to defy the status quo, you and I might not be here today. We must embody, be, and do what Assata Shakur says:

It is our duty to fight for our freedom.

It is our duty to win.

We must love each other and support each other.

We have nothing to lose but our chains.

– Assata Shakur

Writing Prompts to Rise from the Ashes

How are you being silent about your pain?

_____

_____

_____

_____

_____

_____

_____

_____

What does your daring look like, and how can you be more daring?

_____

_____

_____

_____

_____

_____

_____

How are you "coming for" other black women, and why?

_____

_____

_____

_____

_____

_____

_____

What does your rage look like? How does it benefit you, and how does it harm you?

_____

_____

_____

_____

_____

_____

How are you being an accomplice to your own (emotional) murder?

_____

_____

_____

_____

_____

_____

_____

How will you escape the obscenity of whiteness?

_____

_____

_____

_____

_____

_____

_____

_____

_____

How will you dare to rise from your ashes?

_____

_____

_____

_____

_____

_____

_____

_____

_____

_____

"No, I do not yield one second to you!
Not one second."

Maxine Waters

* * * * * * * *

CHAPTER EIGHT

UNAPOLOGETIC

Survival and resistance. Existence as an act of resistance. Black women have learned how to survive in the eye of the treacherous storm that violently tries to destroy them. My mother, born in 1947, grew up in the civil rights era when Jim Crow was as common and natural as breathing. When Rosa Parks refused to give up her seat to a white passenger and Emmett Till was murdered, my mother was six years old. When the Little Rock Nine were blocked from entering an all-white school in Arkansas, my mother was ten years old. When Dr. Martin Luther King Jr. was arrested in 1963 and wrote his infamous Letter from Birmingham Jail, my mother was sixteen years old. And in 1968, a year before I was born, Dr. King was assassinated, and Shirley Chisholm was the first black woman elected to the U.S. Congress (and in 1972, the first black woman to run for president). My mother is alive today. She survived. She resisted.

Rosa Parks didn't apologize for being sick and tired of yielding to white folks. The Little Rock Nine didn't apologize for asserting their right to a quality education and disrupting white supremacy. Dr. Martin Luther King Jr. didn't apologize when he seized the Edmund Pettus Bridge. And Shirley Chisholm was unbought and unbossed and didn't even think about being an apologetic black woman. Apologize for what? For choosing to exist without chains? For demanding the end of the dehumanization of black bodies? For calling a thing a thing and holding white folks accountable for their crimes against black humanity? Nah, Sis, ain't no reason for you to apologize for being black, demanding your black rights, taking up black space, or calling out racism and white terror when it happens to you. You can be boldly unapologetic.

One of my mama's favorite sayings is, "Don't start nothing and it won't be nothing." Sometimes I don't understand her and my Gran's aphorisms, but I always understand this one: she says what she means and means what she says, and whoever she is addressing better pump their brakes or else it is about to be on and poppin'. My mama is pretty low-key, but if you push the right button, it's on! She doesn't always raise her voice or even make such declarations, but she is unapologetic when the time calls for it. Growing up in the Jim Crow Era, I'm sure she had to temper her sass and do some shucking and jiving. I imagine all black folks living and resisting during that oppressive time had to shift to survive. And many of us are still shucking and jiving to appeal to the White Gaze.

Shucking and jiving (aka being apologetic and submissive) has been passed down from one generation to the next, partly as a means of survival, and partly because when you don't know better, you can't do better. According to Clarence Major in *Juba to Jive: A Dictionary of African-American Slang*, the phrase "shucking and jiving" dates back to the 1970s and describes behaviors used by Southern blacks to avoid difficulty, to accommodate authority figures, and to prevent physical and psychological beatings. Black folks have learned how to adjust their behavior in the presence of white folks to be more acceptable, to appease them, and to survive the violently oppressive system of white terror. Crossing the street to avoid white people, diverting our eyes, minimizing the space we take up, lowering our tone, carefully choosing our words, and yielding to white folks are just a few of the ways we have shucked and jived over the years in the face of the White Gaze.

How have you shucked and jived in your life? How have you been apologetic in the face of the White Gaze? In what ways are you yielding to the White Gaze? Do you shift and adjust in the presence of white people? Who I am today is certainly not who I was four years ago. And although I have significantly raised my "woke" level since my teenage years, back then I was ignorant and insensitive because of the infection of whiteness and the indoctrination into shucking and jiving. As I shared in Chapter Five, I wielded the weapon of "light-skinned privilege" every chance I got when I was younger, and often against my darker-skinned sisters and brothers. In many ways, I thought I was better than them because of my proximity to whiteness. But now I realize the only proximity to whiteness I had was my lighter skin and being "well spoken." Whatever the hell that is!

I learned to wield my light-skinned privilege vicariously by watching how white folks treated lighter-skinned black folks compared to darker-skinned black folks. And I cashed in on the fool's gold that white folks hand out to unconscious black folks and to folks who crave the approval of whiteness. I had no interest in dark-skinned boys. I was groomed to speak "properly" (aka white) and to look down on black folks who were "ghetto." I could write a whole book about the ways in which my internalized oppression harmed my fellow black people. This dismissive and violent behavior is just another form of anti-blackness. I'm not that person anymore. I refuse to be that person. I know better and work to be better every day. I still slip up and catch myself reaching for my anti-black weapons, but I'm learning to recognize this when it happens and disarm myself.

Every generation in my family shucked and jived, so how could I not? They didn't know any better, so how could they teach me better? I remember going shopping with my mother and grandmother and being given a unique set of "black mama rules" to follow while in the grocery store. You know them rules: Don't touch anything, don't ask for anything, don't be running around the store like a fool (acting like them white kids do), don't make me snatch you up in this store, don't you embarrass me in front of people (white people), and lastly, don't run over the backs of my feet with the cart! And bittersweetly, I spoke these same black mama rules to my son when he was a young boy for the same damn reasons. To keep him safe. And in the black mamas' quest to keep their children safe, they teach them to shift, adjust, minimize, and censor their true black selves. Black mama rules. Did your mother or grandmothers lay down these kinds of rules for you when you were younger?

Y'all know what I'm talking about! It never failed. Every single time I went to the store with them, they laid down the black mama rules, and I knew better than to break them. I was generally a well-behaved child outside of my occasional sprinkles of sassy mouth. So why did I get this lecture before going to the store? These black mama rules were not put in place because I was some out-of-control child.

They were forms of shucking and jiving.
This is what my mother's and grandmother's mamas
instructed them to do as children.

They were standards to keep me safe.

They were rules to minimize the invasive, persistent, and punitive gaze of white folks who couldn't wait for a black child to step out of line or misbehave so they could act like the Permit Pattys and Barbeque Beckys of today (in other words, call security or report us to the store manager). Oh Sis, you and I both know this white woman violence is vintage and vindictive as hell! Just as our mamas taught us how to be safe, white women's mamas taught them how to be dangerous.

White toxic feminism is full of *Weapons of Whiteness:* conscious and unconscious behaviors and words lethally used to deny your existence, stifle your spirit, silence your voice, and paralyze your progress. White women learn and acquire this assaultive arsenal of weapons, which is directly and vicariously taught and passed on by white mothers, grandmothers, sisters, and aunts. White women have been recklessly and unapologetically discharging these weapons against black and brown women for centuries. And they still do.

An unrelenting weapon that is evident but sometimes hard to define is the White Gaze. The White Gaze, as I define it, is when white folks look upon your blackness to analyze, critique, fetishize, and/or quantify your value. The White Gaze is pervasive, intrusive, predatory, critical, and covetous. White eyes ravage the bodies of black folks instinctually. White folks overtly and covertly stare, goggle, gawk, peek, and glare at blackness to evaluate, scrutinize, crave, and rebuke what they see. The White Gaze is not always directly violent, but it is intentional and annoying. So what is the gaze all about? Why do white people do it? The reasons are profound and disturbing, but you can best believe the gaze is not a coincidence. It is willful. It is by design.

The obvious reasons for the White Gaze are pseudo-supremacy, hate, and ignorance. A lot of white folks gaze because they don't like or understand black people. However, just as many gaze from a place of want, crave, desire, wish, and covet. And at the root of these reasons, they want something black people possess. Hasn't that been true since forever? Has there ever been a time when white folks haven't wanted something from our blackness? To own or steal something? To take or consume something? To copy or mimic something? I can't think of a time. It's what they do and who they are. No matter how much evolution occurs within white folks, they have an innate belief that black people owe them something. They believe we are responsible for providing some sort of pleasure or profit to their lives. They often see us as property, a resource, a tool, and a commodity. And it all boils down to their deep belief in their own white privilege and white entitlement. In this case, their "right" to take from blackness without refusal or consequence.

This type of White Gaze is anchored in an aim to possess. It's embedded in a longing for the unattainable. It's entrenched in a physical appetite and an emotional need. This gaze comes from a place of envious desire. This is disturbing. Words like hunger, thirst, yearning, lust, and salivation come to mind for me. How about you? Can you sense the predatory nature in this type of gaze? When white folks want something they desire from blackness, they gaze. When white folks are ignorant about the black existence and experience, they gaze. They gaze for pleasure. Drooling and salivating over our beauty, our voluptuousness, our ingenuity. Our magic. And sometimes the desire is so strong they touch you. The White Gaze undresses you with its eyes and gazes at your black body with sexual desire. White women in particular crave black women for friendships, and so they gaze. They ooh and aah over our black children and want to pet them. And they gaze because they feel it is their right to consume our blackness without permission.

The white imagination about blackness has proven to be lethal to us. In the imagination that fuels the White Gaze, blackness is perceived as abnormal, scary, fascinating, exotic, dangerous, deadly, hypersexual, and infantile. The gaze is slimy and slick. When white folks gaze at you, it makes you uncomfortable. You feel anxious and guarded. There's always an intention of pleasure, profit, or pain in the White Gaze. It's sinister. It always has been. There will, of course, be white folks that read this book, just because they can't help but gaze into black folks' lives. Hey, white folks! I see you gazing here. Stop it. A better use of your time would be to face the ugliness of your racism and pluck it at the root. Then you'll learn to stop peeking into and coveting our black lives!

I've reached a point in my life where I respond to the gaze with, "What the hell are you looking at?" I have made this statement on many occasions, and it always startles white folks. The most common and immediate response to my comment is that look of shock. Then they get pissed. And some have something aggressive to say. Most times they turn red from embarrassment and glare at me like I've done something to them. All of a sudden, they are the ones feeling attacked and threatened because I had the black-ass audacity to confront their predatory peering. And I did it unapologetically. I always will.

My black-ass audacity was in full effect at a Wal-Mart a couple of years ago. In 2017, my mother had to get all the toes of her right foot amputated. She is diabetic and has a history of circulation problems and blood clots, and she has been taking blood thinners for as long as I can remember. For months before her surgery, she complained to her doctor about her painful feet, but he said the pain was due to either gout or diabetic neuropathy. He kept giving her the runaround and didn't take her complaints seriously. Then her foot and toes started to turn black. She was horrified. We all were. And still her doctor of least twenty years, even though he knew her history of blood clots, kept saying it was gout or neuropathy.

As her toes got blacker and the pain increased, my mother's doctor finally ordered an ultrasound of her leg. And sure enough, she had a clot in her thigh that was blocking blood flow to her lower leg and foot. She saw a cardiovascular specialist, and he recommended surgery to insert a stent, with the goal of returning proper circulation to her feet. The procedure was successful to a certain extent. The area between her ankle and the base of her toes improved significantly, and the natural color returned to her foot. But her toes kept getting blacker. The cardiovascular specialist told my mother that if she didn't have her toes amputated, there was a good chance she'd lose her whole foot. As you can imagine, my mother was bewildered by the news. My soul wept for her.

I felt so bad for my mama. Damn! She had spent her whole life scratching and surviving. She had weathered so many treacherous storms while always being kind and loving to folks who weren't always kind and loving to her. Not to mention that my stepfather, Andrew, had passed away the year before. Even I thought, *Damn, will she ever catch a break in life!* She refused the amputation at first, but I had to keep talking to her once again about choosing to live! She cried, cursed, yelled, and screamed for about a week, but then she agreed to the surgery. The surgery went exceptionally well, and the journey to recovery began. I've been my mama's primary caregiver since the surgery. There were times I had to spend the night with her and/or be at her house several times a day to ensure she was eating and bathing.

For months I went to her house to do wound care. It took almost three months, if not longer, before she'd look at her foot. She was so devasted by losing her toes. She was stubborn, verbally combative, sad, angry, and bitter for the first six months of recovery. Hell, I can't blame her! I can't imagine what it was like for her. I had to be extra patient with her, and sometimes I had to unapologetically call her into the space of truth and acceptance. I had to push her to get up and get moving, and to not give up. It didn't matter what I needed to do or what she needed me to do, I was there. Besides my son and his wife, I have been the only child of hers to stand in the gap, to persist when I was tired, and to stand with her when she couldn't stand alone.

That's my mama! She took care of me before I could walk. Fed me. Bathed me. Carried me. Loved and nurtured me. She may not have known how to be physically affectionate, but I sure as hell didn't want for nothing as a kid. My mama has always been there for me, and I will always be there for her. My caregiving included running her errands, picking up her prescriptions, paying her bills, doing her laundry, cooking her meals, and doing her grocery shopping. Yes, I was tired. Sometimes exhausted. But I never let my mama know I was tired. I just kept on doing what needed to be done for her. And I'm so grateful my husband and I raised our son right. He stepped in like a champ and helped lighten the load, often without me asking. Watching him love and care for his grandmother gave me a glimpse of how he will care for me when the time comes. I love the man I created!

Finally, my mother was able to walk well enough so she could ride to the store with me and use the electronic shopping cart to regain her autonomy. We went shopping at Wal-Mart one day, and this was the day I had to unapologetically confront the White Gaze and directly deal with some white woman violence. Remember, my mom is on a fixed income, so she does all her shopping for the month at one time. Her electronic cart was full, plus she had another cart full of items, and I had my own full cart at the checkout stand.

It was crystal damn clear that whoever joined the line behind us would have to wait a bit for their turn to check out. And let me say this: I don't rush through anything to create ease and comfort for white folks. The days of me following the black mama rules are long gone.

A white woman got in line behind us. She was standing directly behind my mom, who was sitting in the electronic cart. I had already loaded my items onto the counter and was finishing up the transaction. I then began to load up the counter with my mom's items from both her carts. As I added the final items and my mother sat in the electronic cart with her back to this woman, I noticed the white woman's gaze. She looked irritated and disgusted. I know that racist-ass privileged look. It was clear she was annoyed that we had so much stuff and that our checkout was taking a long time. When I saw the look on her face, my blood began to boil, but instead of saying anything, I just took my damn time completing my mother's transaction.

The white woman became more frustrated. She was staring, glaring, and smacking her lips. She then had the violent audacity to reach over my mother's back—almost touching my mother in the process—and slam down a loaf of bread. I thought, *Aww, hell no! What the f*ck!* Out loud, I said, "Do you not see my disabled mother sitting there while you're reaching all over her? You are so damn disrespectful, and I will not allow you to disrespect my mother!"

The woman's face turned red and she said, "Well, why is it taking so long?"

I said, "I don't give a damn how long it takes, you will not disrespect my mama!" The cashier, an older white guy, didn't say a word. He just kept ringing stuff up. I finally said to him, "Are you going to just let her talk to us this way?" He still never said a thing.

Meanwhile, the woman was huffing and puffing and slamming more items on the counter with no regard for my mother's personal space.

I usually make a quick assessment of my surroundings when things like this happen to see how many white folks and black folks are in the space so I know how to respond. But on this day, I didn't give a f*ck! I went into unapologetic protection mode. I knew if this situation escalated into something physical, my mother couldn't defend herself. As the woman kept talking under her breath and slamming items on the counter, I said, "The real problem isn't that we're taking a long time, it's the fact that you're racist."

Man, listen. This woman lost her damn mind. She was so astonished I called her a racist, she almost couldn't breathe. "How dare you call me racist!" she said.

I just kept calling her a racist. And each time she escalated more and declared she was not. Finally, she couldn't take it any longer, and she started aggressively throwing her groceries back into her cart while making comments such as, "Go ahead, Sis-ter, keep calling me racist" and "Fine, I'll let you be queen for the day, Sis-ter." When she said the word 'sister,' her voice was so full of sarcasm and mockery, the word came out like it was two words.

I told her, "I ain't your damn sis-ter and I'm a damn queen every day, you better recognize!"

After throwing all her groceries back into her cart, she sped off, yelling, "I'm going to talk to the manager!"

I didn't even care, although I know what "let me speak to the manager" means and what the potential outcome can be when white women are angry. Still, I wasn't backing down. I refused to bite my tongue. I refused to let this white woman disrespect my mother, and I was willing to pay the cost to be the boss of my right to resist the white woman's violence. After she left, I made sure my mom was okay, and I asked the cashier if he was going to tell the truth about what happened.

He finally said, "She was out of line, that's for sure, and you guys didn't do anything wrong."

I thought, *Oh really, Brad. I sure as hell can't tell that's how you feel.*

As we finished our transactions and began walking toward the exit, I saw the woman talking to a man who appeared to be the store manager, and he was. I took my audacious and unapologetic ass right up to them to see what she was saying. Of course, she was lying. Of course, she painted me to be the angry black woman aggressor. And of course, she told him I called her racist. She demanded he reprimand me. I just stood there repeatedly calling her a liar. She was in a full-blown "how dare a black woman call me on my shit" white fragility tantrum. I then told my side of the story and specifically shared how she was treating my elderly mother. At first, I thought the manager was a white man, but then I noticed his name tag, and his name appeared to be Indian. After looking at him more closely, I realized he was a white-passing man of color.

The white woman kept lying. Then she started crying. And I kept telling her she was lying. She finally couldn't take it any longer. Flabbergasted, she stormed out of the store, yelling, "I'm never shopping here again!"

The manager immediately apologized for her behavior and said he wanted to make sure we got to our car safely. He brought up the racist incident that had happened just days before in Charlottesville, Virginia, where a white man deliberately drove his car through a crowd of protesters, killing a woman and injuring several others. The manager wanted to make sure this woman did not commit the same violent act. That's how upset and irrational she was. He offered to escort us out of the store and sit with my mother while I went to get the car.

He stood watch. He made sure we were safe. I asked him about his name. He said he was from India, and that he understood the gravity of racism and what can happen to black and brown folks when white women act out the way this woman did. What can happen when white women use white fragility to get black and brown people harmed. He helped me load the groceries into the car, and I thanked him for his concern. Whew! I was so livid. My mama and I talked about this violent situation on the drive home, and I assured her I'd always protect her. Thank God the manager was not a white man, or a brown man committed to shucking and jiving, because I could be writing a completely different story. A story of possible police brutality and maybe even murder. No joke! This is the danger fragile white women put black women in all the time. The White Gaze is lethal.

* * * * * * * *

I knew the risk I was taking. And in that moment, my preferred response was to fight back. Had I been by myself, maybe my choice would have been different. Maybe not. All I know is that I was not going to let this white woman kill me and say I enjoyed it. I fully exercised my right to be unwavering in my unapologetic-ness by any means necessary. I chose to not let Becky win in that moment. It was one of those sick-and-tired-of-being-sick-and-tired-of-biting-my-tongue-to-keep-white-folks-comfortable moments. I chose to defy that white woman's White Gaze and stand in my *Unf*ckablewith*! I channeled my inner Auntie Maxine with "if you come for me, I'm coming for you" in my heart. I refused to allow this white woman's lethal imagination of us to keep me captive and out of integrity with my right to freedom. It's my right to be free of the White Gaze and the violence it brings. It's your right too. And when they gaze upon you, I hope you unapologetically unleash your version of *Unf*ckablewith*!

The White Gaze causes you to worry, wither, and weather. The White Gaze is a form of captivity. When white folks trap you in their imagination, you never know what will happen. It's dangerous. And if you're silent about your captivity, they will kill you in their mental holding cell and blame you for your death. On the other hand, when I exercise my unapologetic audacity to confront the White Gaze, I am snatching white folks out of their comfort zone. Because of their privilege, white folks assume they will always be safe, and I am challenging that privilege. In one form or another, they've already imagined me as the angry black woman. And because I am not a petite woman, but instead a woman with stature who commands respect and has resting bitch face, I am automatically a threat to them. Especially when I step outside the confining box they've placed black women in. When I challenge their "authority" and their privilege to gawk at my blackness, they become enraged. Because how dare I, a black woman, confront their pseudo-supremacy?

Now their imagination conjures up feelings of vulnerability and fear. They are afraid, and so they enter the white fragility phase. We know fragile white women get black people killed. Because I choose to be free to say what I feel, I am perceived as dangerous to them. Next thing you know, security, management, or the police are called. You know how this can end. And it's rarely a positive experience. The White Gaze puts you in a state of worry if you don't work to free yourself from it. The White Gaze will chip away at your identity, worth, and value if you don't become unbothered by it. The White Gaze will cause you to weather and become exhausted if you don't defy it. And to that I say, DAMN THE WHITE GAZE!

This is why you must truly understand the root and intention of the White Gaze and how it is trying to captivate you and kill you emotionally. Additionally, it is important that you know who you are, and that you know your value and worth. You must be solid in your identity. Because when you know who you are, you know who you are NOT.

You are not a commodity to be bought.

You are not a problem to be solved.

You are not a project to be completed.

You are not a freak show on display.

You are not eye candy.

You are not someone to fetishize.

You are not abnormal.

You are none of the things that white folks imagine you are. You are whoever the hell you say you are! And you must be utterly unapologetic about who you are, without hesitation or concession.

A first step in liberation and shutting the blinds on the White Gaze is to know yourself, identify yourself, and be solid in your identity. Sis, Audre Lorde sums this truth up perfectly when she says, "*If* I didn't d*efine myself for myself*, I would be crunched into other people's fantasies for me and eaten alive." The White Gaze is hungry, and it will eat you alive if you let it. A second step in starving the White Gaze is to move through the world with your Unf*ckablewith vibe. When you navigate spaces where white folks exist, you gotta be completely and unapologetically unbothered by their perceptions about your blackness. They must become virtually invisible to you. It's your right to move through the world without the gawks, glares, and gazes of white folks. Don't give them your precious life source. Starve the f*ck out of them.

Move through the world like Maxine Waters! Do not yield. I absolutely adore Auntie Maxine Waters. I have a feeling that if, God willing and I get to her age, I will be as feisty as she is. If my Aunt Bobbie were alive today, I suspect she'd be just like Maxine Waters, utterly unapologetic as f*ck! Auntie Maxine gives zero f*cks about that damn White Gaze and the words that come out of racist white folks' mouths.

The fearlessness Auntie Maxine embodies in the face of hate, discrimination, and scrutiny is refreshing and empowering. She's been categorized as unruly and turbulent. She's been threatened and retaliated against, and still she rises! Not giving a damn about what people say, she stands her ground and refuses to allow other folks to dismiss, demean, or dehumanize her. When folks try to burn her and set her on fire, she always emerges from the ashes like a black phoenix and becomes the fire. In my opinion, Auntie Maxine is the epitome of Black Woman Badassery. She is undeniably Unf*ckablewith and I'm here for all of it. All the time. You can always count on her to reclaim her time and her power because she knows who she is, and she refuses to let other people define her and dictate how she shows up in the world.

Know thyself. Identify thyself. Value thyself. Unapologetically. This is essential to your survival. Unapologetically owning your black unbothered existence is foundational to your resistance. This is how you rise from the ashes. It's a pillar in positioning yourself to thrive. Go forth, Sis, and unleash your unapologetic black woman badassery. You have a duty to fight for your freedom. You have a duty to win. You have nothing to lose but your chains. And as you fearlessly go forth, remember this when you encounter the White Gaze:

I don't owe white folks a hello.

I don't have to smile.

I don't have to be friendly.

I don't have to concede.

I don't have to submit.

I don't have to respond.

I don't have to shuck and jive.

I don't have to get out of the way.

I don't have to accommodate.

I don't have to shift.

I don't have to explain.

I don't have to beg.

I don't have to shrink.

I don't have to watch my tone.

I don't have to settle down.

I don't have to apologize.

I don't have to agree.

I don't have to play nice.

I don't have to conform.

I don't have to keep the peace.

I don't have to teach.

I don't have to make white people comfortable.

I don't have to grin and bear it.

I don't have to tiptoe.

I don't have to be silent.

I don't have to.

And I won't.

Be unapologetic!

Go ahead, Sis. If you like, channel your inner Auntie Maxine Waters!

"I'm a strong black woman and I cannot be intimidated.
I cannot be undermined."
– Maxine Waters

Writing Prompts to Rise from the Ashes

What does your resistance look like?

_____

_____

_____

_____

_____

_____

_____

_____

_____

What are you unapologetic about?

_____

_____

_____

_____

_____

_____

_____

_____

_____

What privileges do you have, and how are you using them to harm other black women?

_____

_____

_____

_____

_____

_____

_____

What do you do when you encounter the White Gaze?

_____

_____

_____

_____

_____

_____

What are you willing to do to pay the cost to be the boss?

_____

_____

_____

_____

_____

_____

How can you use your right to be unapologetic to get and live free?

_____

_____

_____

_____

_____

_____

_____

_____

_____

_____

How will you unapologetically rise into your black woman badassery?

_____

_____

_____

_____

_____

_____

_____

_____

_____

_____

ANGELA DAVIS

REVOLUTIONARY

"I am no longer accepting the things I cannot change. I am changing the things I cannot accept."

Angela Davis

* * * * * * *

CHAPTER NINE

REVOLUTIONARY

What would the state of black women be without our ancestors? Would we be the women we are today without the black women revolutionaries who came before us? Where would we be without the tireless and relentless resistance of Shirley Chisholm, Fannie Lou Hamer, Sojourner Truth, Angela Davis, and Harriet Tubman? All the black women who came before us—known and unknown, family members and complete strangers—paved and continue to pave the way for our liberation. I always knew they were phenomenal and powerful women, but today this truth is not only anchored in my soul, it is also fuel for my fire. When the world tries to consume me, I remember these women and what they did for humanity and justice, and I remember that I, too, am phenomenal and powerful. And when the world tries to set me on fire with its violence, I can rise from the ashes and become the fire. And so can you!

The courage, tenacity, and fearlessness Harriet Tubman displayed in every rescue mission—at a time when death without trial was the norm—was revolutionary. She had a target on her back and a bounty on her head simply for exercising her human right to be free. Harriet was determined to disrupt the system that shackled the feet of her people, and she dared to liberate black folks by putting her own life in the line of fire. Each remarkable rescue attempt was the ultimate act of defiance black folks could commit back then. Nothing enraged white folks more than an uppity negro who took her freedom into her own hands and outsmarted the so-called "superior" race. The audacity of this black woman thinking about freedom, let alone achieving it, made white folks' blood boil. Harriet was a disrupter. Harriet was a dramatic changemaker. She was a revolutionary. A radical, rebellious, black woman.

Harriet Tubman paved the way and kicked the door open to the liberation movement before the infamous words "by any means necessary" were uttered by Brother Malcolm X. She was the embodiment of unflinching courage in action, and she defied the odds to demonstrate hope for black freedom. Harriet may not have been the first black woman to spark the liberation movement, but she lit that thang up, leaving a blaze of flames behind her badassery and illuminating the path for other black women to carry the torch of freedom and liberation!

Flash forward to 1970, and picture the big-ass afro and raised black fist of Sister Angela Davis. A warrant for her arrest was issued after the Marin County courthouse incident, in which Jonathan Jackson, the brother of George Jackson (one of the three Soledad Brothers), attempted to take hostages in exchange for the Soledad Brothers' release from prison. A superior court judge and three others, including Jonathan Jackson, were killed. Angela was not directly involved in the crimes, but she was accused of being an accomplice to conspiracy, kidnapping, and homicide because the guns used in the incident were registered in her name. She fled to avoid being arrested and was placed on the FBI's Ten Most Wanted Fugitives List. Several months later, she was captured in New York, and she was acquitted on all charges in 1972 after spending over a year in jail.

Angela Davis was not just a high-profile case, she was an activist for black liberation, and thus someone the system wanted to make an example of. The system was relentless in persecuting and prosecuting this black woman as a scare tactic to force black folks to shut up and stay in their place.

How dare a black woman in the 1970s, only a few years after the passing of the Civil Rights Act, speak truth to power?

How dare she call a thing a thing and try to hold the system accountable for its crimes against black humanity?

How dare she speak up about the violence against the black community and demand that it end?

A black woman. A bold black woman. How dare this black woman be strong, articulate, persuasive, and unapologetic? How dare she try to exercise her right to be free and unchained! Angela continued the revolution. Angela is a revolutionary. And through her books and lectures, she is still a vital part of the black liberation movement.

Both Harriet and Angela were revolutionary, but what does that look like today? Sadly, the revolution for black freedom and liberation is far from over. And as far as I am concerned, to be black and a woman is all it takes to be a revolutionary. Our daily need to resist oppression, and our will to exist despite that oppression, is a revolutionary act. The word "revolutionary" means a radical, rebellious, dramatic changemaker who disrupts the status quo. Do you favor or work toward drastic social or political change? Do you defy or resist authority or tradition? Do you act to disrupt oppressive systems? Yes? Then you, by definition, are a revolutionary.

I think some folks don't want to label themselves as revolutionaries because it can seem arrogant. I can dig it. I'm sure neither Harriet nor Angela ever used the word to describe their unflinching dedication to black liberation—well, maybe Angela did. Whether you choose to see yourself as a revolutionary or not, one thing is undeniable: every black woman who defies societal expectations, and who disrupts the systems and ideologies trying to smother her voice and keep her captive, is a revolutionary.

I don't know about you, but I choose to be a revolutionary. When I examine the gifts my creator has put in me, the personality planted inside of me, and the passion and love I have for people, black people, and justice, I can't help but be a revolutionary. I also choose to define what "revolutionary" looks like for me and how I will embody it and activate it in my life. My version of revolutionary is encompassed in something I say often: "Live free or die trying." The courageous act of striving to live free in a society that oppresses women and blackness is an act of defiance. It's revolutionary. Every day, I consciously choose to speak my mind, even when I'm afraid. I take up my rightful space and let people know when they are invading my space. I walk with my head held high like I deserve to be here, because I do. Essentially, I do everything that whiteness says I shouldn't do without its permission. To me, being a revolutionary means to defy expectations at every turn, especially those mandated by whiteness.

I'm not afraid to be radical. I'm not afraid to rebel. I am very comfortable disrupting the status quo by how I think, speak, act, show up, navigate, and educate. This is me walking in my version of revolutionary. I've mastered being *Unf*ckablewith*. I've defined myself for myself.

I'm comfortable being an agitator and a disrupter. I'm not afraid to create waves, and I'm not afraid to walk alone while doing so. This is my personal revolution.

What are you unafraid of?

How are you comfortable showing up?

How will you show up more radical, rebellious, and disruptive?

How do you walk in your version of revolutionary?

* * * * * * *

I shared this quote by Audre Lorde in the previous chapter, but it bears repeating here: "If I didn't define myself for myself, I would be crunched into other people's fantasies for me and eaten alive." We're all going to leave a legacy when we die. That legacy can be consciously or unconsciously determined, so why not be intentional about how you choose to show up in the world? Are you trapped in other people's fantasies of you? Perhaps you're trapped in your own untruth. Maybe you've been trying to live up to the standards and expectations of friends and family. And maybe you're showing up the way you think the world wants you to show up.

To paraphrase Lorde: Have you defined yourself for yourself? Or are you allowing the expectations of others to eat you alive?

You don't have to label yourself a revolutionary, yet it is imperative you fight not only against the systems that oppress you and others, but also against those that deny humanity the right to be free and to thrive. I love and agree with what Audre Lorde said in her speech "Learning from the 60s," which she delivered at the 1982 Malcom X celebration at Harvard University:

You do not have to be me in order for us to fight alongside each other. I do not have to be you to recognize that our wars are the same. What we must do is commit ourselves to some future that can include each other and to work toward that future with the particular strengths of our individual identities. And in order to do this, we must allow each other our differences at the same time as we recognize our sameness.

—Audre Lorde

The speech ends with this important message:

As Malcolm stressed, we are not responsible for our oppression, but we must be responsible for our own liberation. It is not going to be easy, but we have what we have learned and what we have been given that is useful. We have the power those who came before us have given us, to move beyond the place where they were standing. We have the trees, and water, and sun, and our children. Malcolm X does not live in the dry texts of his words as we read them; he lives in the energy we generate and use to move along the visions we share with him. We are making the future as well as bonding to survive the enormous pressures of the present, and that is what it means to be a part of history.

—Audre Lorde

Black woman, you are walking history and creating it with every choice you make. Are you going to let the world define you, or will you define yourself? Are you going to let people kill you, and you'll say you enjoyed it? Are you going to let the hunters tell your story, or will you tell it yourself? Listen, you may not see yourself as a revolutionary, but if you define yourself, refuse to let people kill you, and tell your own story, that is revolutionary!

What you do today and in your lifetime will help create the conditions for future generations of black women. The freedom and rights we have now are because the black women who came before us said yes to being their own version of revolutionary. And just like we are our ancestors' wildest dreams, future generations will be our wildest dreams. What's your dream for future generations? What would you like them to be able to do after you have taken your last breath and are long gone? What would you like future generations of black women to experience that would call you to rejoice from the grave?

My Aunt Bobbie, she was a revolutionary, but I never heard her say the word. She loved black people. After deep reflection, I realize just how pro-black she really was. I never understood her bouts of callouts to white folks. I remember being with her numerous times out in public when she would become so annoyed with folks who stared at her. I guess that's where I get my "what the hell are you looking at" sass from, because that's what she would say to white folks who gawked at us while we were shopping. And when she did, I'd be taken aback and mesmerized by her ferocity. I was too young to truly understand the dynamics of the situations, but one thing is for sure: I admired her fight, her feisty, and her fearlessness.

My auntie was like Shug Avery from the movie *The Color Purple*, and I was like Celie, always following her and wanting to be wherever she was. My auntie was a pistol, and she was unwavering in speaking her truth. She was fascinating. I was often captivated by how she chose to show up in the world despite her personal struggles. She was not to be messed with, and everyone knew it. She loved her some me, and I knew that too. I realize now I loved being with Aunt Bobbie because she spoke my language. A language I had yet to fully express and master. A language of truth and freedom I admired. A language deep down inside of me waiting to come out. And although I knew better than to speak it at a young age, I would secretly think, *Oh, I can't wait until I can speak like that.* Back when I was young, I didn't know what a muse was, but my auntie was certainly my muse.

I can't count the times my mother would tell me I was radical and arrogant when I was growing up. I didn't know what she meant by "radical." And I often thought, I'm not arrogant, I just say what I mean and mean what I say. I don't think she used the right word to describe my sass. Folks didn't really use the words "unflinching" and "unapologetic" back in the day. Was I arrogant? I don't think so. At least not the way I define arrogance. Was I unflinching and unapologetic? Yep! I came out of the womb that way. When I would get sassy with my mother, she'd say my mouth was going to get me in trouble one day. I really didn't believe her. Because in my mind I was not only being true to myself, but also speaking my truth.

My sass was constant throughout my time in elementary, middle, and high schools. If there was one thing I got in "trouble" for, it was saying what was on my mind. And often I didn't do it in a disrespectful way, but nevertheless, my teachers despised the audacity of a black girl who was unafraid to call out injustice, unfairness, and disrespect. I couldn't help it. It's as though my soul carried the eyes of justice, and when I saw injustice, I had to speak on it. I didn't have the language back then to explicitly define the Weapons of Whiteness I teach about today, but my soul knew black and brown bodies were being violated by those weapons. I could clearly sense and feel the marginalization and humiliation my fellow black and brown classmates experienced because of the treacherous words and actions of white teachers.

This discernment and fine-tuned empathy I embodied for humanity was still taking shape in my younger years. This was an early example of my claircognizance and clairsentience abilities I mentioned in Chapter Six. I've always known I have the innate ability to read between the lines. The ability to dissect people's words and actions to find the truth under the veil. The ability to sense how others are feeling and the compulsion to do something about those feelings. I call them "bread crumbs," and I'll tell you why.

Do you know the story of Hansel and Gretel? Hansel and Gretel were the children of a poor woodcutter during a time of famine. Their mother plotted to take them into the forest and leave them there to fend for themselves. Their father was reluctant at first, but eventually agreed to go along with the horrible plan. Hansel and Gretel overheard the scheme, so Hansel went outside and gathered as many white pebbles as he could. The next day, the mother and father took the children into the forest. As they walked, Hansel dropped pebbles on the ground, leaving a trail. After their parents abandoned them, Hansel and Gretel found their way back home by following the white pebbles. When the mother realized they had returned, she became angry and locked them in their room.

The next day, the family took another walk in the forest, and once again, the mother planned to abandon Hansel and Gretel. This time, Hansel grabbed a piece of bread before they left and dropped bread crumbs to mark their trail. But birds ate the crumbs, and Hansel and Gretel got lost in the forest. Finally, they stumbled upon a large cottage made of gingerbread, cakes, and candy. Tired and hungry, they approached the house and began to devour it, not knowing it was a trap built by a blind witch who used it to lure children into her home.

The blind witch captured Hansel and Gretel. She turned Gretel into her slave and locked Hansel in a cage with the intention of fattening him up so she could eat him. Hansel and Gretel eventually outwitted the witch, pushed her into a hot burning stove, and grabbed precious stones they found in a vase as they were escaping. Their father was overjoyed when they returned home; he had regretted his decision to abandon his children, and their mother had died of unknown causes. Now wealthy due to the witch's stones, the woodcutter and his children lived happily ever after.

I share this story to help illustrate something I talk about frequently. I believe the soul knows, and it knows the way. I believe each of us is born with a unique purpose. Some people hear the word "purpose" and believe it has to be some gigantic and grandiose endeavor or task. That is not always the case. We're not all meant to be superstars, celebrities, and Nobel Peace Prize winners. Some of us are not meant to be in the spotlight; instead, we are meant to be the wind beneath other people's wings. No person's purpose is too big or too small. We all matter. And we are all here to do two things for sure: to love and to serve, and to serve in the way we were designed to serve. I also believe a divine entity, I call it "God," implants our purpose while we're in the womb, and we come into this world innately equipped to fulfill that purpose.

I tend to agree with Doris Lessing when she talks about how we are briefed on our purpose shortly before birth:

God gives us the brief before our birth, before our soul's descent into flesh. But after our births we remember the briefing only dimly, because taking on a body weakens the ability of the spirit to remember who we are and what we're here for. So, the nagging sense of having forgotten something important, the longing without cause, the calls that haunt us like whispers from a little too far away, come from our remembering parts and fragments of the briefing. The calling is not forgotten entirely, but it is muted and fuzzy, like a distant radio station whose signal is filled with static.

—Doris Lessing

I also agree the calling is not really forgotten. Hansel and Gretel's pebbles and bread crumbs are the whispers Doris talks about in this passage. Faint yet real beckonings from your soul; whispers that say, "Come home!" And for me, "home" in this illustration is your soul. Your soul already knows who you are, why you're special, and what purpose you're here to fulfill. You may think you've forgotten your purpose, but all you need to do is look for your pebbles and bread crumbs. And if you can't find them, don't worry! After all, Hansel and Gretel finally found their way home, but not by using the pebbles or bread crumbs. Instead, they outwitted the witch. You too will still find your way home to your soul, your true essence, your calling, your destiny, your revolution—whatever that is for you—with or without the bread crumbs and pebbles.

In Chapter Six, I described the encounter I had with the palm reader. I knew she was right about my purpose because I had been feeling as if I had forgotten something important. I felt a longing without a cause, and I kept hearing the nagging whispers (and sometimes the bonks upside my head!) from my creator, nudging me to come home to my calling, my purpose. There had been many bread crumbs and pebbles along the way, including my gifts of discernment and fine-tuned empathy for humanity I mentioned earlier, that I hadn't known how to follow. I still wasn't sure how I was going to find my way home, but it was clear what home was for me. This racial justice work I do is my purpose, my calling, my unique work to do. Coming home to it has satisfied my soul in a way no job ever could. I am so grateful to be home. I'm overjoyed, and my soul is on fire for this work, for my purpose. And I will choose to create my happily ever after as it suits my desires.

Once I finally returned home, I knew I had to unleash my *Unf*ckablewith* and become the fire, because when I had done this work under white folks' mandate, they tried to kill me. I refuse to die this way. I choose to be free and do my work my way, or to not do it at all. I also strategically and intentionally designed my version of this work to be radical, rebellious, and revolutionary. And no matter how many black women did this racial justice work before me or how many do it after me, no one, absolutely no one, will ever do it like I do it. The way I embody my resilience, ingenuity, and magic cannot be duplicated. I am unbossed and unbought. I am *Unf*ckablewith*. Every day I rise from the ashes into my black woman badassery!

Sis, you are the revolution. You are part of the collective black revolution. I encourage you to go home. And if you're already home, stay there. There's no place like it. Find your way back to your soul's purpose. Your destiny and fulfillment lie there waiting for your return. Go, Sis. Don't let them kill you. If you're sitting in ashes right now, trust and believe there is *Unf*ckablewith* inside of you too. Unleash that shit and rise into being your own kind of revolutionary. Rise high and strong into your black woman badassery!

Writing Prompts to Rise from the Ashes

Which black women do you think are revolutionaries, and why?

_____

_____

_____

_____

_____

_____

_____

_____

How do you define "revolutionary"?

_____

_____

_____

_____

_____

_____

_____

_____

_____

What is your purpose?

_____

_____

_____

_____

_____

_____

_____

What whispers are you hearing right now?

_____

_____

_____

_____

_____

_____

What do you want your legacy to be?

_____

_____

_____

_____

_____

_____

_____

What does your soul crave?

_____

_____

_____

_____

_____

_____

_____

_____

_____

_____

How can you use your own version of revolutionary to rise from your ashes?

_____

_____

_____

_____

_____

_____

_____

_____

_____

_____

"Truth is powerful and it prevails."

Sojourner Truth

* * * * * * * *

CHAPTER TEN

TRUTH

Ain't no badass like a black woman and that is the truth! Black women are a revolution all by their damn selves. And black women have paid the cost to be the boss. Black women have fought and died to gain every civil liberty known to humanity, but even after the passing of the Civil Rights Act of 1964, black women in America must still fight for freedom, liberty, and justice. And I imagine black women all over the world are fighting for something, because if they are black and they are women, they are fighting misogynoir, anti-blackness, and colorism on some level. With *everyone*, including other black women, coming for us, I know you're fighting at least one fight, if not several. And no matter how badass you are, you've got to take care of yourself by putting yourself first. You must begin and/or continue to be true to who you are. To live *your* truth.

When I think of the word "truth," a few synonyms come to mind, such as fact, real, certainty, accuracy, honesty, and veracity. The one word that encompasses all these words for me is "authenticity." Authenticity is undisputed realness. It cannot be replicated or duplicated. And it cannot be confiscated. That's my favorite. Can't nobody steal your authenticity. It's your magic, Sis, and no one can take it from you. They may try to copy it, but you are one of a kind. Your authenticity is the truth of who you are. Your authenticity is meticulously coded into your DNA. It's perfectly imperfect. It is a divine inscription from your creator. Your authenticity is your default status. It's the internal software that came with you, and it cannot be disabled.

But as with any software, there can be malfunctions, viruses, and bugs that interfere with and slow down your authenticity code. Life, stress, oppression, racism, financial challenges, mental health issues, and toxic people will fragment your system and cause you to be in a state of dysfunction and distress. All these challenges have one intention: to disable you and force a shutdown. How are you protecting your authenticity? And what are you doing to combat the viruses and bugs that attack the truth of who you are? As Sojourner Truth said, "Truth is powerful and it prevails." Listen, all those outside attackers have one goal in mind, and that is to take away your power and keep you from prevailing. Your truth is under attack.

Our truth—as we define it, embody it, speak it, and live it—is all we have. When you relinquish your truth and authenticity, what are you left with? Your truth is sacred. It is divine. It is powerful. You must unleash it. Cultivate it. And protect it. What is your truth? What is undisputedly real about you? If you're like me, you've been infected with the lethal virus of whiteness, and it has affected your default status. Growing up in a society that has deep disdain for blackness takes a toll on your truth. From a young age, white lies are fed to you in every way, shape, and form. And after years of this deadly diet, after years of you digesting and metabolizing this poison, it can slowly damage your magic.

I've talked a lot about knowing thyself. I realize some of you have had your ancestral and cultural identity stolen; I know this because it is true for me too. I've always wondered what my African ancestral roots were. And over the past four years, there's been a clear and profound whisper from my ancestors telling me to come home to the truth of who I am. Every year since 2010, I've been choosing one word to use as my vision and guide for how I want to experience life that year. In 2011, my word was "truth." I chose truth because at that time in my life, I felt like I was wallowing in a bed of lies. Lies other people were telling me. Lies people were hiding from me. And lies I was believing and telling myself. I was desperate for the truth.

Once it was clear that "truth" was my chosen word, I made a list of all the lies I was wallowing in and the truths I needed and wanted so I could be in integrity with myself. And at the top of the list was my desire to find out who my biological father was. All my life, my mother had told me my father was a man named Tony, and I believed her. I also believed he was a jerk for not claiming me and being in my life. Tony has a son who is just a few days younger than I am, and that son happened to be a junior and senior high school classmate of mine. It saddened and infuriated me to see Tony always showing up to school events for his son, but not showing up for me. I carried a lot of resentment toward him in my younger years.

By the time I was in my early thirties, I began to work on releasing this pain and sadness, but there was always an empty space in my heart. A space of unknowing. I finally reached a point of forgiveness not only for Tony, but also for my mother. Because I have to admit there was a part of me that was angry with her for choosing him to be my father. I know that sounds ridiculous, but it's true. I realized just how ridiculous this resentment was when I got pregnant with my son by Marcus (not his real name), a man I liked. Marcus turned out to be kind of like Tony. The only difference is Marcus claimed my son, partly because my son resembles him, so Marcus couldn't deny him. But Marcus was willfully absent for most of my son's life, and still is. I tried so hard to keep my son connected to his father and never closed the door, even though I had a man in my life and my son had a stepfather. It didn't matter. Marcus chose to not walk through the door for whatever reasons.

Now I was in my mother's shoes. I had chosen an irresponsible man to be the father of my son, and I had quite a bit of regret and guilt about that. When I say "choose," I don't mean I purposely picked him for that reason, but I did choose to have unprotected sex with someone I liked a lot. I wondered if my son would resent my choice like I had resented my mother's. After I had my son, I realized I needed to forgive her, and I realized that no woman can make a man be a father against his will. Lord knows I tried. Perhaps my mother did too. I could empathize with her, so I had to release the resentment I felt—for her sake and my own. And I did.

However, I still wanted to know whether this Tony guy was my father. He looked like he could be. Not necessarily his actual features, but because my mother is much darker than I am, I knew my father had to be very light or possibly part white. Tony was half-black and half-Italian, and over the years, several people in my hometown would say, "You may not look like him, but you sure do look like his sisters." I saw one of Tony's sisters at the grocery store one day when I was in my early twenties, and they were right, I did look like her. I also had (and still have) a compelling attraction to all things Italian, so I chalked this fascination up to it being in my DNA. I thought maybe I was part Italian too. A huge part of me believed he was my father, but in 2011, I needed to know for sure.

One day, I searched for Tony on Facebook. I ended up finding someone with his exact name, but this young man looked mostly white, as some of Tony's other children do. The only way you can tell they are one-fourth black is by the texture of their hair. I knew Tony had a son (my former classmate), so I figured this young man must be Tony Jr. I courageously messaged him, saying, "Let's connect, I might be your sister." I worried he was going to think I was strange and/or that my message was a hoax, but he responded right away and informed me he was indeed Tony Jr., Tony's son. I asked him if he would send a message to his dad asking him to call me. I was afraid Tony Sr. would ignore my request, and the pain of abandonment would be compounded. But he didn't. He called me that same day.

Tony and I talked over the phone for hours, sharing stories, asking questions, and fact-checking, so to speak, about the potential of him being my father. He said he wasn't sure he was, but he was willing to take a DNA test, and he offered to pay for it. I was shocked and relieved, and I accepted his offer. I took the lead in finding a credible testing site near my home town in Iowa and scheduled the appointment. We agreed I would drive to my home town and then we'd take the thirty-minute trip together to the diagnostic center. The anticipation leading up to the meetup was killing me. I wondered what I'd do if he was my father. I wondered what I'd do if he was *not* my father. At the end of the day, all that really mattered to me was discovering the truth. I was ready for and needed this truth in my life.

On a spring day, I made the drive and met Tony at a local convenience store. He got out of his truck to greet me. We hugged, hopped into his truck, and headed to the diagnostic center. I remember staring at him intently, or as much as I could without being intrusive, to see if I could recognize myself in him. This was the first time I had been up close and personal with the man I believed to be my father. The more I observed him, the more I knew in my gut he was not my father. He was a nice man. He was kind, generous, and compassionate. We talked, shared more stories, and laughed during our ride together. At the center, we checked in, and they took us to a room to explain the procedure. After we signed the necessary paperwork, they performed the test by swabbing the insides of our cheeks for samples to send off to the lab.

I remember having a deep exhale on the ride back to my car. I knew the truth was soon to be revealed. Tony asked me if I wanted to have lunch once we got back to the city, and I said yes. We had a great time talking, and he seemed very interested in me, my family, and the vision and goals I had for my life. He shared more about his life, and we both agreed we'd be okay with whatever the results were. I'll never forget him saying he hoped I was his daughter because he thought I was a brilliant and phenomenal woman. While I wanted this to be true, my gut just knew it wouldn't be. And I was right. Two weeks later, I got the test results in the mail, and they read, "Zero percent chance that Tony *last-name-withheld* is your father." I cried.

Even though I knew this would be the result, I was tired of wondering. I wanted this part of my journey to be over. I didn't want to search anymore. I wanted to close this chapter of my life for good. After gathering myself, I called Tony and shared the results. He was silent. And when he eventually spoke, he said he was very sad to hear he was not my father. During the two weeks while waiting on the results, we'd had several enjoyable phone conversations. He was actually a pretty cool guy. And then he took my breath away by saying how much he admired me, and that even though he was not my father, he was willing to be a father to me if I wanted that. And I did. I agreed to stay in contact with him. For the next three or four years, I would call him and wish him a happy

Father's Day, and occasionally he'd call and check up on me. Over the past few years we haven't spoken much, but I am grateful for the moments we shared.

After I discovered the truth that Tony is not my father, I continued to wonder who my father could be. But for about eight years, I stopped focusing on it. Then, in early 2018, I finally did a DNA test to learn more about my African ancestry and with the hope that maybe I could find my father. Although that test provided me with some interesting insights about my ancestry, it didn't reveal the answers I was seeking.

However, later that year, a memory popped into my head. I recalled an occasion in my early twenties when I had been at my best friend Joyce's house. Out of the blue, her mother had said, "You know you're my niece, don't you?" At the time, Joyce and I just laughed off her mother's statement because she was quite tipsy from drinking. I never forgot the moment, but I also didn't act on it until the memory resurfaced in 2018.

I don't believe much in coincidences. I knew this memory was coming back to me for a reason. So I acted on it; I called Joyce, and I asked her if she would do a DNA test and told her why I wanted to do it. Ever since we became best friends in high school, I have been deeply and strangely connected to her and her family. They felt like family to me, and I spent more time with them than I did with my own family. I ordered the test, and when it arrived, Joyce came to my house and we did it together.

Several weeks passed. I really didn't think too much about the results. I figured it had to be a long shot, yet there was a tiny piece of me that knew her mom had called me her niece for a reason. And then that day happened! I will never forget that day, the day I was driving around running errands, and I got a text from Joyce that said, "What up, Cuz!" Cuz as in cousin! What the hell! I screamed in my car. I was so flooded with joy and tears I had to pull over to the side of the road. I couldn't believe it. I immediately called Joyce and said, "Is it true, are you my cousin?" She said, "Yup, we are first cousins." I cried. I sobbed. I balled. I exhaled. It was cleansing and cathartic. I couldn't contain it. My eyes are filled with tears right now as I write this chapter.

After celebrating with my best-friend-now-cousin Joyce over the phone for about fifteen minutes, I sat on the side of the road and cried some more. I thought I had healed my daddy wound, but now I realized just how much I had needed to know the truth. And I did know the truth. I knew immediately it was true, that Joyce's uncle was my father. And while this was a moment of tremendous joy, it was also a moment of breathtaking sadness. Because Joyce's Uncle Buddy (my father) had died many years before. I had finally learned who my father was, but I would never get to know him. He had passed away when I was about nine years old.

I sat in the car and continued to cry. This time I cried tears of sadness, realizing I'd never meet him, and he'd never know I was his daughter. I kept crying. And cried some more. And at the same time, I rejoiced that I had been with my family all along. I hadn't known, but God had. Finally, after forty-eight years, I know who my father is. His name was Lee Smith Jr., and he was also known as Buddy. The truth was revealed, and although I will never get to know him, I now know WHO I am and where I come from. I also discovered I have an older sister named Lisa, who lives in Oklahoma, and two nieces with children. I plan on meeting them in person real soon. Whew! What a journey. Sojourner is right, the truth is powerful, and it will prevail. The truth is cleansing, healing, cathartic, and empowering. And it will set you free!

Searching for and leaning into the truth about my father has given me a greater sense of freedom. I feel like a ton of anxiousness has been released, and most importantly, I know who I am. *Knowing* who you are is liberating and *accepting* who you are is revolutionary. Who are you? Do you know who you really are? Are you connected to your truth, your identity, and your cultural and ancestral roots? What is your truth? I believe we all crave truth and desire it to be a central part of our lives. I mean, who wants to live a life full of lies or based on lies? I don't, and so much so that truth is one of my top five core values, along with authenticity, freedom, peace, and inspiration.

I conclude that Sojourner Truth, feminist and abolitionist, was craving some truth too. She was born into slavery in rural New York in about 1797, and she was bought and sold four times during her lifetime. New York slaves were emancipated in 1827; the year before, Sojourner Truth ran away from her final "master" with her infant daughter, Sophia, to a nearby abolitionist family, the Van Wagenens. They bought her freedom for twenty dollars, and they helped her sue the state of Alabama for the return of her five-year-old son, Peter, who had been illegally sold into slavery. Twenty dollars! Twenty damn dollars. Ain't that some sadistic shit! The price white folks put on our lives back then is atrocious, and sadly, I bet if they could put a dollar amount on our lives today, it wouldn't increase by much.

* * * * * * *

After Sojourner became an itinerant preacher, an evangelist preaching about affliction and redemption, she met with abolitionists such as Frederick Douglass to give speeches about the evils of slavery. She eventually went on to give speeches about human rights for women and blacks, including her infamous "Ain't

I a Woman" speech in 1851, in which she declared race and gender should not prevent women from voting. Sojourner Truth was one of the first true intersectional feminists who paved the way for future generations of black feminist women. One thing I so deeply appreciate about Sojourner Truth is she took back her sovereignty by releasing the slave name that stole her authenticity and truth. She knew she wasn't no damn Isabella! Just like I know the name "Catrice Jackson" is not true to my ancestral authenticity. I plan to release the slave masters' grip on my sovereignty one day soon by changing my name.

What's in a name anyway? Everything! Whether we choose it or it's given to us, I believe there is power in your name. Still, what's truly important is not what they call you, but how you identify yourself and what you answer to. In my journey to reclaim my ancestral sovereignty, I also took the African American Ancestry DNA test and discovered my matrilineal ancestry is rooted in Cameroon. I AM Cameroonian! You have no idea how long I've waited to say who I am beyond "African American." Finding out this piece of my stolen ancestry has been liberating and cathartic. It has emboldened my authenticity and how I show up in the world as a Black African woman. The best part of this specific DNA test is that it was created explicitly for black people. It helps us not only identify our country of origin, but also the specific ethnic tribes we come from. I am from the Mala, Tikar, and Kotoko tribes of Cameroon.

As I type these tribe names, I raise my head high and I feel black-ass pride in my back. I'm smiling on the inside, and my ancestors are celebrating as I reclaim who I am. They are cheering me on, saying, "Yes, Sis, stand in your glorious ancestral power!" I know they are with me, and I know I am their wildest dreams. The oppressive lies are being shattered, and as each one crumbles, I care less and less about the violent white gaze. I care less about what other people think about me. I care less about conforming to the status quo. I'm releasing the world's expectations of what it means to be black and a woman, to be a black woman. This is my truth. This is my authenticity. I am reclaiming my ancestral sovereignty and feeling more *Unf*ckablewith* with each new discovery. And to that I say, "Yes, Sister Lorde, I am defining myself for myself, because I refuse to be eaten alive by whiteness and societal fire."

You know, maybe being *Unf*ckablewith* as I've described it in this book is not for you. Maybe you have your own version of what it means to be unbothered by the white gaze and unapologetic about your blackness. That's cool. I respect that. And no matter how you define discovering and living your no-permission-needed truth, I support you. In whatever way you choose to live YOUR truth, do it your way. That's what it means to be *Unf*ckablewith*! I just have this hope for you: that you deeply realize the healing power embedded in this personal work, your journey to living free and being liberated from every false depiction, harmful affliction, and oppressive restriction that is trying to keep you from your truth and that is trying to kill you.

The lies you've been told, the poison you've been fed, the direct racial trauma, vicarious racial trauma, generational trauma, and all the maladaptive circumstances you've experienced in your lifetime have been strategic and intentional. These are the trap doors the system of whiteness has perfectly constructed for your demise. And within these trap doors are hallways of regal regeneration and revolution. Sacred spaces to reclaim your sovereignty. There are rooms you must enter for your soul healing. Because the circumstances you've been through have created soul wounds.

Many people believe trauma is in our thoughts and memories, and it is, but it is primarily housed in our souls. When you are harmed, abused, and oppressed, the residue of the trauma remains in your soul even when the scars go away or you forget them. Have you ever thought you were over some pain or bad experience, and then something occurs that triggers a negative response? For example, you go through a bad breakup with a lover, and you think you've gotten over it, but then someone brings up their name or you see them, and you instantly become angry, sad, or lash out. These responses are signals that the wound has not healed. These are trauma responses, and they are signs you have more work to do to heal that wound and release that toxicity from your body. You think you've done the work, but your soul knows the truth and remembers the pain of that relationship.

Let me be clear. Soul work and soul healing are not easy, but they must be done. As always, you can choose to not do the work. But why cheat yourself out of experiencing the best life possible? You deserve that. It's your right. And the responsibility to create and cultivate your best *Unf*ckablewith* life is up to you in spite of the fire and the storms. Your ability to truly thrive depends on your willingness to recognize and name the pain you feel, to accept that it's real, and to be unwavering in your healing. One thing I know to be true is that the system of whiteness wants you to remain scared, sick, hurt, wounded, and broken. It knows that if you are healed, happy, and harmonious within, then you are a powerful force to be reckoned with. A revolutionary force.

Sis, it's time to set yourself free from your own captivity. By "captivity," I mean self-doubt, anger, pessimism, jealousy, resentment, self-loathing, confusion about who you are, and any other challenge that steals your joy and paralyzes your progress. And yes, I am exceptionally aware of the external cages the world has (or tries to) put you in. I'm redirecting you back to you, your body, your soul, and the work you can control. I know many of those external oppressions are out of your control. This, what I'm talking about right now, is YOUR work to do. And no one can do this work but you. There are a lot of strategies and techniques out there that will help you begin your healing work, too many to name.

I want to share what I think is the most powerful first step in your healing journey, and this comes from my twenty years of experience as a Licensed Mental Health Clinician and Counselor. Truth. Your truth. Unfiltered. Raw. Explicit truth. Tell yourself the truth. You can't change what you're not willing to address, and you can't heal something you refuse to name. By allowing whatever pain or hurt you have in your soul to remain, and telling yourself that you're fine and it's okay, is to lie to yourself and be completely out of integrity and soul alignment. The soul knows the truth, and therefore, this discomfort or dis-ease is stored in your body, not your mind. The real wound is a soul wound, which means cognitive interventions will not be your most effective options for healing.

What I mean is, yes, talking to trusted friends and going to therapy will help with some of the symptoms of the pain or wound, but the real work has to be done via body work. Because that is where the trauma is housed: it lives in the body and reverberates into your emotions and mind. After telling the truth and owning your pain and/or wounds, the second step I encourage you to take is to choose healing. And choose it relentlessly and repeatedly. I want you to choose it like you choose to breathe. Choose it like it is the most important thing you'll ever do in your lifetime, because it is.

Choose yourself over everything.
Choose your health and joy before you choose others.
Choose life.
Choose freedom.

Choose liberation.

Choose to be happy.

Choose to be whoever the f*ck you want to be. Healing is not optional.

I don't have a perfect prescription for your soul healing. However, I believe the best approach for most black women is to participate in both mental health therapy and body work (alternative healing modalities). There are many forms of body work, and you don't always need to pay someone for these services. A few therapeutic examples are massage, aromatherapy, acupuncture, cupping, yoga, hot stone therapy, reflexology, Reiki, herbalism, meditation, and sound and color therapy. Others may include visualization, guided imagery, music and dance therapy, artistic expression, and of course, nutrition. Listen to your body and soul; they know what you need.

I am a proponent of talk therapy and/or cognitive behavioral therapy, and I have practiced this methodology myself with great outcomes. If you choose to include mental health therapy as part of your healing work, it's critical you hire a therapist who is culturally competent and who understands the impact of racism and oppression on the lives of black women. Before you hire someone, make sure they are doing their own anti-racist work and they have a tangible anti-racism plan as part of their service provision. I cannot stress this point enough. If you do not hire someone with these qualifications, and do not hire someone who uses a trauma-informed method of treatment, you will be retraumatized, and your soul wounds will be exacerbated. Please do your due diligence if you decide to pursue mental health services in your community.

And while I agree cognitive behavioral therapy is helpful and therapeutic, I don't believe it's enough on its own. I am coming to understand just how important alternative healing modalities are, such as the ones I mentioned above. I encourage you to choose the modalities that feel good to your spirit and that will produce the best results possible. Personally, I am a fan of body massage, as it literally reduces pain and tends to move painful (negative) energy out of the body. I do not claim to be an alternative healer of any sort; instead, I am offering you information that may be of value to you. Participate in these types of healing modalities at your own risk, and be sure to do your research before you choose practitioners.

What has become clear to me, and what I believe, is that soul healing is essential for black women. It's critical that we each choose the best methods for our own healing. You have to do what is right for you. And I'm on my own journey of soul healing. I'm realizing the significance and value in reconnecting to what was lost or stolen from many black people, including our ancestral roots and spirituality, and our ancestral healing modalities and rituals. Reconnecting to our ancestral roots also requires learning the truth about who our ancestors were and are. Do you know who your ancestors are? Are you connected to them? Are they part of your daily life?

One piece of my healing journey has been the relentless pursuit to discover who I am and who I belong to. As I mentioned earlier, in June of 2018, I did an African American Ancestry DNA test and it revealed to me my origins, my soul home, and my tribal brothers and sisters. This has been very cathartic and healing. Finding out who my father was and discovering my unique ethnic tribes has been salve for my soul. I'm still exploring my tribes and learning more about the ways in which I can walk in the truth of who I am and be authentically true. It's a moderately expensive test, but the fruit of the investment is priceless. It was important for me to know the truth, my truth, and maybe it is for you too.

My third suggested step for your journey is for you to define and embody liberation and revolution on your own terms. You've mastered your ability to be resilient and strong; now it's time to master your ability to heal and thrive! I hope this book, with its stories and suggestions on how to be *Unf*ckablewith*, have inspired you to define and embody what being *Unf*ckablewith* means to you. You must live in your authenticity and in the truth that you are free and liberated. How you do it doesn't matter to me—I just want you to be *Unf*ckablewith*! My desire for you is that you will be unbothered and unapologetic. That you will rise from the ashes into your Black Woman Badassery. That you will relentlessly activate your Black Girl Magic to resist, rise, revolutionize, and thrive.

And my final wish for you is this:

It's okay to be soft, to surrender, and to be vulnerable.

Tell yourself the truth.

Live your truth unapologetically.

You are the revolution.

Be your own kind of revolution.

Find your way home. Your soul knows the way.

Reconnect to your soul's purpose. Fulfill your destiny.

Go forth. Unbothered. Unwavering.

Don't let them kill you.

Refuse to retain and transmit trauma.

Detoxify your soul from the White Gaze.

Damn that White Gaze!

Those ashes ain't got shit on your Unf*ckablewith!

Transcend the storms.

Rise up and regenerate, Black Phoenix!

Be black. Be whole. Be healed. Be free. Be liberated!

Activate your melanin magic!

Thrive!

Shine!

Do not let the fire burn you.

Become the fire and blaze up.

Activate your black girl magic.

Rise. Thrive. Shine.

– Catrice M. Jackson

Writing Prompts to Rise from the Ashes

What is your truth?

_____

_____

_____

_____

_____

_____

_____

_____

What truth do you need to discover?

_____

_____

_____

_____

_____

_____

_____

_____

Do you have mommy or daddy wounds? If so, how are you healing them?

_____

_____

_____

_____

_____

_____

_____

What has whiteness stolen from you?

_____

_____

_____

_____

_____

_____

Have your ancestors been nudging you to hear and act upon some truths?

_____

_____

_____

_____

_____

_____

How would your life improve if you began living your truth?

_____

_____

_____

_____

_____

_____

_____

_____

_____

_____

How can you use truth to rise from your ashes?

_____

_____

_____

_____

_____

_____

_____

_____

_____

_____

* * * * * * * *

A LOVE LETTER TO BLACK WOMEN

As a straight, black, able-bodied, formally educated, light-skinned, financially secure, Midwestern American woman, I'm fully aware of the seats of privilege I sit in and the perspective from which I see the world. My perception is my reality, and my reality provides the ink from which the words in this book flow. And I am aware that the words chosen to express my thoughts and truth are the fruit of my privilege and illustrate my experience. Because of my privilege and perspective, I don't know your particular truth and reality, and I don't claim to. Yet I want to understand it as much as I can. I don't know what it is like to be queer or non-binary. Yet I am working to learn more every day. I don't know what it is like to have limited physical abilities or to experience mental health issues. Yet I strive to be empathetic, supportive, and nourishing.

Maybe some of the things you read in this book didn't sit right with you, or maybe you didn't agree with them. Maybe I could have said things a different way. Maybe you were annoyed by something I expressed in this book. And maybe my perspective on blackness wasn't global or inclusive enough. I'm not sure what you might be thinking. But it is important for me to share with you my awareness of my perspective and privilege as I put these words to paper. I want you to know that even if I didn't get a point across the way you might have liked me to, I was conscious while creating this work, to the best of my wokeness or consciousness at this moment. I want you to know I'm on my own personal journey of evolution; just like you, I am working on evolving into a better woman, a better soul, a better human.

I realize some of my suggestions and strategies might not be right for you, or they might not work for you. Yet I believe they can work for those who are able to carry them out. After I finished this book, I asked myself, "Is it complete? Did I say everything I wanted to say? Is there something missing?" I originally had a different vision for this Afterword, just as I had a different vision for the book cover. But in the thirteenth hour, just days before my deadline, spirit spoke to me and said, "Change it. Change the book cover." And so I did. I listened to the one voice that drowns out the rest—my God, my creator—and was obedient to the demand. The same is true for this Afterword. Spirit spoke and said, "Write a love letter." So here I am expressing my deep love for you, Black Woman.

Everyone in the world is coming for you. You've got people's feet on your back, your neck, and every part of your beautiful black body, trying to hinder, stop, or kill you. I personally understand the weight and burden of being a black woman, even though I'm very different from you, and you are very different from me. I also know that when the day finally comes when black women are thriving, the whole world will thrive. I often say the worst betrayals are those committed by one black woman against another black woman. It's true. For me, anyway. Because we know the struggles of being a black woman. We know the pain of misogynoir. We know the sting of anti-blackness. This healing and liberation work aren't only an individual thing. It must be a conscious collective action.

Dr. Martin Luther King Jr. said, "An individual has not started living until he can rise above the narrow confines of his individualistic concerns to the broader concerns of all humanity." I translate this to mean that for black women to heal individually, we must also commune to heal together.

And in order for us to effectively commune for healing and liberation work as one collective body, we must be willing to admit our mistakes, acknowledge our shortcomings, respect and honor one another, listen to one another, and love each other through the journey. On this journey, we must hear each other, forgive each other, and hold each other in high regard even when we disagree. You may be saying, "Catrice, that's hard to do." And it is. I believe you, because I too struggle with this sometimes, especially when I've been betrayed by my sister. Yet we must be there for each other. If we aren't, who will be? We're all we've got!

By no means am I asking you to let other black women walk all over you and to turn the other cheek. However, I am asking you to give your sisters, black women, as much love, grace, and compassion as you'd like to be given. That's all. And if by chance you encounter a black woman who you just don't jive with, release her with love. Let her go. Do no harm and love her from a distance. I've had to do this and will do it again if necessary. There is no need to bash and trash another black woman. I am sure she gets plenty of that from everyone else. Don't be a source of pain for another black woman. Be a solution or set her free.

And while I understand that people who are hurting are the ones most likely to hurt others, using your trauma as a weapon against other black women is not only harmful, it's self-abuse. When you hurt your sister, you hurt yourself. None of us are perfect. But we all matter. You matter. We all have our shortcomings, yet I'm adamant that each of us, that you, have the capacity and the power to not only heal your own life, but to also be the balm for other black women. Yes, I want you to put your oxygen mask on first, and then, within your capacity to love, help another black woman breathe. Put your self-respect at the top of your daily to-do list, and let's do away with the respectability politics. Because respectability politics are killing us, as is our enactment of them.

June Jordan says, "I must undertake to love myself and to respect myself as though my very life depends upon self-love and self-respect." I agree. I know you want to help your sisters. Perhaps you are helping them already, and you want to do better or offer more. That's lovely, but you can't pour from an empty cup. I hope this book inspires and equips you to fill YOUR cup. And I hope your cup is not only filled, but that it also overflows with love, forgiveness, grace, and compassion for your fellow black women. Take care of yourself, Sis, and then serve other black women from your rich, abundant overflow. I believe that healing begins where self-love and self-respect lives. Healing is an act of love. Do you love yourself enough to heal? Do you love black women enough to help them heal?

Healing is liberation. Healing is freedom. I want you to be and live free! Although Assata says we have nothing to lose but our chains, and I agree, I also believe Nelson Mandela's words: "For to be free is not merely to cast off one's chains, but to live in a way that respects and enhances the freedom of others." You can't be truly free if your sisters are still in bondage. We get free together, and we do it by any means necessary. We do it with arms locked, feet planted, wounds healed, minds made up, and with an *Unf*ckablewith* spirit. And we don't stop. We won't stop until we all are healed, liberated, and free. Fannie Lou Hamer was right when she said, "Nobody's free until everybody's free." Let's get free together. It will be imperfectly perfect!

The current narratives of black pain and bondage are not how our story ends. There's more. You are not the person other people have told you that you are. The legacy you leave behind is still unfolding and taking shape. In your pursuit of the path and embodiment of being *Unf*ckablewith*, you can write a new story. You can rename yourself and redefine yourself. You can change what you see before you. You can reclaim your sovereignty and sacredness. You can choose healing and liberation. This is not the end. We're just getting started, Sis, and once we start together, it will be on and poppin'! And you can rise from the ashes of everything trying to take you out, into your most spectacular and majestic version of black woman badassery.

There are really only two true emotions: love and fear. And then there are all the variations or shades in between. Simply put, feelings or emotions that constrict, agitate, irritate, and/or create tension, such as anger, sadness, and hate, are variations of fear. On the other hand, feelings or emotions that expand, amplify, soothe, and nourish, such as joy, peace, and happiness, are variations of love. Take some time to examine the feelings and emotions you experience the most, and you'll soon discover whether you are existing in and operating from spaces of love or fear. This awareness, and intentionally doing your own personal work to shift into and exist in more spaces of love, is healing work. Love is healing, and healing is love. I hope you love yourself enough to heal, and that you love your sisters enough to help them heal. Healing is not optional if you truly want to thrive.

Sis, I love you. I want you to heal. I want you to be liberated and free. I love you enough to walk this journey with you. I hope this book and its message have been healing balm for your soul and fire in your belly. I hope you choose to be *Unf*ckablewith* on your own terms. And let me end by declaring this truth: ain't nothing like an *Unf*ckablewith* black woman! Healed. Free. Liberated. Imperfectly perfect. Badass! Rise up, Sis, like a black phoenix. Become the storm. Unleash your black woman badassery. Let the healing begin. Liberate yourself.

I love you, Black Woman!

* * * * * * *

THREE POWERFUL STEPS FOR YOUR HEALING JOURNEY

Tell Yourself the Truth
The Unfiltered. Raw. Explicit truth.

* Tell *yourself* the truth.
* You can't change what you're not willing to address, and you can't heal that which you refuse to name.
* By allowing whatever pain or hurt you have in your soul to remain, and telling yourself that you're fine and it's okay, is to lie to yourself and be completely out of integrity and soul alignment.
* The soul knows the truth, and therefore, this discomfort or dis-ease is stored in your body, not your mind.
* The real wound is a soul wound, which means that cognitive interventions will not be your most effective options for healing.

Choose Healing

* The real work has to be done via body work. Because that is where the trauma is housed: it lives in the body and reverberates into your emotions and mind.

* Choose it relentlessly and repeatedly. I want you to choose it like you choose to breathe. Choose it like it is the most important thing you'll ever do in your lifetime, because it is. Choose yourself over everything. Choose your health and joy before you choose others. Choose life. Choose freedom. Choose liberation. Choose to be happy. Choose to be whoever the f*ck you want to be. Healing is not optional.

* There are many forms of body work, and you don't always need to pay someone for these services. A few therapeutic examples are massage, aromatherapy, acupuncture, cupping, yoga, hot stone therapy, reflexology, Reiki, herbalism, meditation, and sound and color therapy. Others may include visualization, guided imagery, music and dance therapy, artistic expression, and of course, nutrition. Listen to your body and soul; they know what you need.

* If you choose to include mental health therapy as part of your healing work, it's critical you hire a therapist who is culturally competent and who understands the impact of racism and oppression on the lives of black women. Before you hire someone, make sure that they are doing their own anti-racist work and they have a tangible anti-racism plan as part of their service provision.

* If you do not hire someone with the above qualifications, and do not hire someone who uses a trauma-informed method of treatment, you will be retraumatized, and your soul wounds will be exacerbated. Please do your due diligence if you decide to pursue mental health services in your community.

Define and embody Liberation and Revolution On Your Own Terms

* You've mastered your ability to be resilient and strong, now it's time to master your healing and ability to thrive!

* As long as you live in your authenticity and in the truth that you are free and liberated. How you do it doesn't matter to me—I just want you to be *Unf*ckablewith*!

* My desire for you is that you will be unbothered and unapologetic. That you will rise from the ashes into your Black Woman Badassery.

* That you will relentlessly activate your Black Girl Magic to resist, rise, revolutionize, and thrive.

* * * * * * * *

WEAPONS FOR WINNING

(AGAINST BECKY)

Weapons for Winning and Amplifying Your Joy

When Becky comes for you with her Weapons of Whiteness, you can stand firm in your *Unf*ckablewith* using these Weapons for Winning. You can read more about these weapons in my book *The Becky Code: How to Deal with White Woman Violence While Amplifying Your Joy.*

1. **DARE to Speak:** When white women DENY your truth, stories, and experiences, DARE to speak and call them out on their violation and violence. Of course, you must DISCERN whether this is a battle you're willing to engage in or not. If you decide it isn't, remember your silence will not protect you. If you fail to address Becky's violence, she is likely to violate

you again. Iyanla Vanzant says, "We must call a thing a thing." This means you must identify and name racism for what it is by calling it out explicitly as White Supremacy.

2. **DISOBEY the Expectations:** When white women DEFEND their racism, they expect you to stay silent and to accept their manipulative, defensive rationale. They expect you to understand their "mistake." They expect you to talk nicely to them about your pain while they cause it. They expect you to pull them to the side and to not call them out publicly. They expect you to NOT shame them. They expect you to forgive them for their violence. They expect you to watch your tone and to not be angry. They expect you to explain or teach them about racism. DISOBEY ALL THESE EXPECTATIONS!

* DO NOT let them take your kindness for weakness.
* DO NOT subdue your tone and voice. Remember what Zora says!
* DO NOT feel the need to talk privately about their racism. They will abuse you behind closed doors.
* DO NOT let them manipulate you with declarations of shame and their white tears.
* You DO NOT have to forgive their violence.
* DO NOT waste your magic and emotional energy on educating them.
* Be angry and mad if you want to. You DO NOT need anyone's permission or approval to express your anger. (Don't stay angry, however, because doing so hurts only you.)
* DO NOT FOLLOW THEIR RULES OF ENGAGEMENT. DISOBEY EVERY TIME. For centuries, white folks have had

the expectation that black and brown folks will follow their white rules and expectations. You don't have to!

3. **DISCONTINUE the Dialogue:** When white women try to DERAIL the conversation about racism, know this is an intentional tactic used to avoid looking at their own racism. White folks get extremely uncomfortable when talking about racism, and they will try to create an intellectual and emotion distraction to avoid dealing with their passive or active role in racism and white supremacy. Instead of following them into the violent white abyss, call out their attempts to derail the conversation. At this point, Becky has made it clear she does not want to hear your truth, and she does not want to stop her racial violence. DETACH. It's time to DISCONTINUE dialoguing with her. This is not a battle you want to continue. It's at this point that we give away our precious energy and power to antagonistic white women who do not want to change. Walk away. You do not have to prove your humanity to them. They are NOT worth the agony.

4. **DETOX and Delight:** When white women try to DESTROY your joy, say, "Nah, not today, Becky!" On some days, it is worth the fight to go into battle with Becky. But I want to encourage you to choose a different, more nourishing option instead on most days. When the need arises, then dare to speak, disobey the expectations, discontinue the dialogue, and demand to be heard and respected. And don't forget to maintain your magic by detoxing yourself from the Beckyism. You are here for a very special reason and a divine purpose. Don't let Becky hijack your destiny! Taking care of yourself and making YOU priority number one is essential.

* * * * * * * *

UNLEASH YOUR MAGIC
WHAT IS MAGIC?

LIST AND EXCERPT FROM THE BECKY CODE.

* Magic is turning your words into experiences.
* Magic is moving a dream from distant thought to an intimate reality.
* Magic is making the invisible tangible and touchable.
* Magic is predicting how your life turns out.
* Magic is transforming your physical body and restoring your vitality.
* Magic is purging your soul from everything that paralyzes your purpose.
* Magic is doing work you love and loving the work you do.
* Magic is leaping out of your comfort zone into the unknown and thriving.
* Magic is turning limiting beliefs into limitless possibilities.
* Magic is creating harmony within and living your own unique melody.
* Magic is creating and experiencing moments that take your breath away.

* Magic is trusting that your soul knows the way and following it.
* Magic is saying "so what" and living your life unapologetically.
* Magic is slowing down and savoring the silence and synchronicity of life.
* Magic is hearing the whispers of the divine one and saying "yes!"
* Magic is unleashing your gifts and serving the world with them.
* Magic is not giving a damn what other people think of you.
* Magic is making a meaningful contribution to humanity.
* Magic is fiercely loving you better than anyone else ever could.
* Magic is following your bliss and wallowing in all the goodness and splendor you can imagine.
* Magic is having peace of mind, love in your heart, and a generous spirit.
* Magic is deeply forgiving yourself and choosing to love and be loved again.
* Magic is being comfortable in your own skin and appreciating every magnificent part of yourself.
* Magic is thinking positive thoughts and showing up in the world with optimism.
* Magic is curiosity, creativity, and answering your life's calling.

Magic is unlimited! There are so many ways to create magic in your life in your own unique way. Please stop trying to duplicate someone else's life. You'll never live their dreams. You'll never walk their path. You'll never carry out their purpose, and you'll never arrive at their destination. Embrace the awesomeness of your originality, manifest your own dreams, confidently walk your own path, and live out your special destiny that's designed just for you!

* * * * * * * *

50 WAYS TO BE MORE COURAGEOUS

Here are 50 tips for you to live more courageously, from my book *The Art of Fear-Free Living: Awaken the Geni(us) Within.*

1. Make a list of the things you need to forgive yourself for, and then, one by one, release the shame, guilt, and regret.

2. Identify the people in your life you need to forgive. Choose to do the work within your heart to forgive them.

3. Start a courage journal, write down all the things you want to do, and find creative ways to make them happen.

4. Choose the risks you can take now to be more courageous.

5. Remember not only the moments when you were wise and strong, but also how you were able to create success in those moments.

6. Make a list of the values and standards you want to live by, and start living by them. For some ideas to get you started, see the "Words to Inspire Your Core Values" section in this book.

7. Think about all the things you do that you don't like or want to do and create your "not to do" list. Once the list is complete, be brave and just stop doing those things.

8. Use your fears to drive you toward your passion and purpose.

9. When you become aware of fear, remember that the awareness of fear is a signal that something is missing from your life.

10. See the same significance in feeding your soul as you do in feeding your body. Determine how you will feed your soul every day.

11. Check your emotional energy tank and determine who is filling it or causing you to run on fumes. Determine what you can do to remove the energy stealers in your life and do it.

12. Decide what you can do every day to move from surviving in life to thriving in your life.

13. Every time you feel fearful, ask yourself, "What is the worst that could happen if I do not face this fear, and what is the worst that could happen if I do face this fear?" You'll see you have more to lose by NOT facing your fears.

14. Remember, you have only two choices in life: be afraid and live afraid or be fearless and live courageously.

15. Instead of focusing your energy on your fears, focus your energy on how you can get the resources you need to conquer the fears.

16. Color the canvas of your life with vibrant, energetic, and happy people who can keep you inspired to master the Art of Fear-Free Living.

17. Remember that every day you have the choice to take down the old, dull, and gray canvas and put up a blank one to create your fearless life.

18. Know that your personal power is like a big eraser. You have the power to erase the negative thoughts about yourself. Erase the past hurts that are keeping you stuck. Erase everything in your life that is causing you distress and misery.

19. As you begin to create a fear-free life, remember that you have the tools you need within you—you just have to seek them out and use them.

20. Be mindful to stay off autopilot. Instead, live each moment of your life fully awake.

21. Make it a personal priority to ask yourself every day, "What d I need to face, and how can I face it not only with the resources I need, but also with ease and grace?

22. Be intentional in every moment. Engage only in activities and conversations that move you one step closer to your goals.

23. Remember that facing your fears is simply about taking risks. You must be willing to take some risks to get what you desire.

24. Create a vision board, and fill it up with words, pictures, and quotes that depict how you want to live your fearless life.

25. Create your fearless life dream team: a small group of dedicated, positive, and trustworthy people who believe in you and your dreams and who will help you bring them to life.

26. Be mindful to not make excuses or reasons for not doing something that can empower your life. Excuses are the doorway to failure.

27. When faced with a fear, instead of allowing yourself to worry and become paralyzed, seek out the resources to help you conquer the fear.

28. Be curious. When faced with a fear, ask yourself, "I wonder what would happen if I faced this fear?" Be still and listen for the answer that comes from your heart.

29. Make the choice to accept that you will have obstacles in your life and begin to see them as opportunities to strengthen yourself.

30. Instead of dreading facing your fears, wake up each day with gratitude and ask yourself, "How can I be brave today?" And then take action.

31. *Unsubscribe!* That's right; opt out of everything that does not fill your cup, fulfill you, serve your highest good, and/or take you one step closer to your highest self.

32. Surrender once a day. In the morning, surrender to the Universe and let God order your steps. In the evening, surrender again and release all the toxicity you've taken in during the day.

33. Choose to be struggle-free! Pay attention to the moments where there is struggle and decide in the moment that your life is not worth the pain and frustration that struggle brings.

34. Be accepting. Sometimes you've simply got to say, "It is what it is." Let it go and keep it moving.

35. Quit looking for the answers. Instead, choose to allow them to just come to you, and enjoy life while you wait for the divine downloads to occur.

36. Trust yourself more. Trust that what you need will come. Trust that you know yourself better than anyone else. Stop fighting with yourself, and instead, just trust yourself.

37. Take action! Worrying, contemplating, agonizing, and analyzing are signs of struggle. Ask your heart and your soul whether you should act, and if you feel peace overcome you, then get out of your head and take action.

38. Learn how to filter out the background noise. The background noise is other people's opinions, demands, and requests. It's your life, do what you want to do, and make your own decisions.

39. Release the need to be right or perfect. There's no such thing as perfect, and you will never be right all the time. Instead, strive to be the best you can be without measuring yourself against anyone. Remember that being wrong means you're human.

40. When you stop judging others, you will learn to accept them for who they are. This allows you to begin to accept yourself just as you are.

41. Your past is a part of who you are, but it does not determine who you will become. Let go and be free or keep holding on and be miserable.

42. Take out a new canvas every day and start over. Yesterday is gone and is a memory. Tomorrow may never come and is a dream. Today is all you have and is a blessing.

43. Every day you have a choice to stay captive, or to be brave, take out your courage key, and unlock your life. Stop wallowing in "what if," and begin basking in your bravery.

44. Look for at least one opportunity each day to grow and evolve. Read a new book, write in your journal—it doesn't matter what you do, as long as it takes you one step closer to fearless living.

45. Get over yourself! Someone out there has it worse than you do. While you are indeed important, the world does not revolve around you.

46. Fearless living is about survival of the fittest. Either you change, grow, and evolve, or life will pass you by. Get up and get into your life.

47. You can't change everything in your life with one choice, but the choice to live fearlessly can dramatically change your life.

48. Choose to live deliciously! Write down your recipe for a delicious life on a real recipe card. Get creative and add in a little spice, passion, excitement, satisfaction, and zest, and you are sure to whip up a life that makes your mouth water.

49. Clock in and go to work! Living YOUR LIFE fearlessly is an inside job. It's the most important job you will ever have in your life. Go in early, work hard, take on extra projects, be on the leadership team, put in 100%, stay late, clock out, and start all over again. When you work this job like it's the only one, you'll ever have, the recognition, raises, and promotions are guaranteed.

50. Decide what you want, how you want to be, and how you want to live your life, and then get it, be it, and live it. The only thing keeping you from living a rewarding and fulfilling life is you. Tell your ego to get out of the way and allow your best version of yourself to reign in your life. It's your life—own it, create it, live it, and love it—fearlessly!

* * * * * * * *

WORDS TO INSPIRE
YOUR CORE VALUES

One of the ways that I stay grounded in my truth and remain *Unf*ckablewith* is establishing and living by five core values. I use these values as the foundation for how I choose to show up in the world and as guiding principles for how I want to live my life. My core values are *Authenticity, Freedom, Truth, Peace*, and *Inspiration*. I've been using these five words to navigate my best life since 2010. I encourage you to choose five foundational words that best represent the core of who you are and how you want to navigate your life. The words you choose should serve as the pillars to your unwavering way of being and represent the truth of who you are. Here are few words to inspire the creation of your core values. This list comes from my book *The Becky Code*.

Creativity	Inspiration	Fantasy
Innovation	Focus	Meaning
Fascination	Glory	Curiosity
Serendipity	Exploration	Love
Vibrancy	Magnetism	Peace
Gratitude	Joy	Abundance
Prosperity	Security	Safety

Laughter	Excitement	Adventure
Compassion	Passion	Faith
Serenity	Purpose	Clarity
Optimism	Determination	Grace
Courage	Bravery	Appreciation
Beauty	Contribution	Satisfaction
Service	Generosity	Empathy
Wisdom	Belief	Happiness
Fun	Connection	Trust
Flow	Synchronicity	Harmony
Intention	Luxury	Truth
Magic	Vitality	Play
Aliveness	Relaxation	Imagination
Confidence	Delight	Leisure
Freedom	Calmness	Authenticity
Audacity	Resiliency	Ancestry
Impact	Discipline	Sovereignty
Justice	Tenacity	Transformation

* * * * * * *

ABOUT THE AUTHOR

CATRICE M. JACKSON, MS, LMHP, LPC

CATRICE M. JACKSON is the Global Visionary Leader of the Awakened Conscious Shift, the CEO of Catriceology Enterprises, LLC, an international speaker, and a best-selling author. Catrice is passionate about empowering people and making an impact in the world. She's a humanist and activist dedicated to social and racial justice, because without either, people cannot fully or rightfully thrive in life. As an educator, consultant, and speaker, Catrice blends psychology, social consciousness, racial justice, and leadership wisdom into meaningful messages that propel people into action. Catrice is a dynamic difference maker with a voice that's unflinching, authentic, and powerful. She is the catalytic creator of SHETalks WETalk Race Talks for Women and WETalks for Women of Color. Catrice is strong medicine and serves up hard truths necessary to eliminate the lethal infection of racism from humanity. She realizes that her approach may be rebuked and her flavor undesired. Catrice knows she is not for everyone and that everyone won't like her, and she is unbothered by both. She is unmoved by naysayers and does her work authentically and unapologetically with a revolutionary spirit and believes that justice is love.

For as long as I can remember, I've always had something to say. I'm often compelled to speak up for the underdog and about the injustices in the world. I have a passion for raising difficult topics and engaging in courageous conversations, conversations that challenge "the way things are" and help transform lives. I value truth, freedom, authenticity, courage, and peace, and I intentionally infuse my core values into every human engagement, keynote speech, training, and workshop and on any platform for which I am called to be a voice.

Empowering the lives of people is my passion. I'm on a relentless mission to make a difference, to do work that is meaningful, and to inspire others to use their gifts for social change. I believe justice is love in action, and I'm committed to loving on humanity by being an activist for racial justice. I'm here to challenge the status quo, to disrupt injustice everywhere, to dismantle systems of oppression, and to wake people up into an awakened, conscious way of being, living, and engaging.

EDUCATION

* PhD, Organizational Psychology, Walden University (dissertation in progress).

* MS, Human Services/Counseling, Bellevue University. GPA 3.97.

* BS, Criminal Justice Administration, Bellevue University. GPA 4.00 (dean's list).

* Licensed Practical Nurse, Western Iowa Technical Community College.

* Certified Domestic Abuse and Sexual Assault Advocate, Trainer, and Speak

CATRICE M. JACKSON

* * * * * * * *

SOCIAL MEDIA CONTACT

Facebook
@CatriceJacksonSpeaks
@blackwomanbadassery

Twitter
@Beckyologist

Instagram
@Catriceology

YouTube
@Catriceology1

RADIO
SHETalksWETalk Radio
blogtalkradio.com/shetalkswetalk

WEBSITES
www.catriceology.com
www.catriceologyenterprises.com
www.shetalkswetalk.com
www.thebeckycode.com

HIRE CATRICE FOR SPEAKING AND EDUCATION
Catrice is also available for speaking opportunities, radio and podcast segments, organizational training, anti-racism education, and leadership consulting.

* * * * * * * *

OTHER CATRICEOLOGY BOOKS | All Books Sold on Amazon

The Becky Code
White Spaces Missing Faces
Antagonists, Advocates & Allies
Unleash Your Significance
The Billboard Brand
Brand Like A BOSSLady
The Art of Fear-Free Living

UNF*CKABLEWITH

Rising From the Ashes Into Your
BLACK WOMAN BADASSERY

56921491R00162

Made in the USA
Columbia, SC
02 May 2019